I0827972

How to build a better spouse trap

How to choose a mate, learn from your mistakes, stay married, and teach others to break the cycle of dysfunctional relationships.

Hollis L. Green, ThD, PhD

a division of
GlobalEdAdvancePress

How To Build a Better Spouse Trap
How to choose a mate, learn from mistakes, stay married, and teach others to break the cycle of dysfunctional relationships.

Library of Congress Control Number: 2010925290
Green, Hollis L., 1933 –
How to Build a Better Spouse Trap

ISBN 978-1-935434-45-0

Subject Codes and Description:
1: FAM030000: Family Relations: Marriage 2: REL 001205: Religion: Christian Life – Love and Marriage; 3:JNF053020 Social Issues: Dating and Sex.

Printed in the United States of America

Published by

Marriage and Family
an imprint of
GreenWine Family Books

This Book is
Affectionately dedicated to colleagues

STEVE AND MARIA CECILIA MOHAMMED

Who constantly work with couples to build strong
Marriage and family relationships
Through Campus Crusade/FamilyLife.

CONTENTS

The marriage relationship must grow with tender loving care!

...it helps to have a mature hand to guide the young in search of an acceptable companion.

Author's Preface

Conversation is key to a workable relationship. There must be dialogue, mutual exchange, general discussions, small talk, quick chats, and long term one-to-one, heart-to-heart exchanges to make a marriage work. Only this process can bring about true respect and love in an extended relationship.

How it all began!

Seeing a young lady in church without a man for several weeks, I became interested. Observing her devotion, her interest in music, her involvement with children, and her general demeanor, my heart spoke to me. I think it was my heart, maybe it was my mind, or even my aloneness. Regardless, when one gets a message from the inner self, it has a compelling voice that demands action with objectivity.

The church where this happened was near Dobbins Air Force Base in Georgia. She was never with a man, so my curiosity was aroused. Being a reserve Chaplain with the USAF, I thought perhaps her husband was in the military, maybe on a Temporary Duty Assignment somewhere. Surely, such a marvelous lady would not be without a man!

Planning to leave the area for a speaking engagement, My inquisitiveness wanted to know whether or not she was engaged or married, or otherwise committed to someone. At the close of a church service, I went up to her and asked, "Do you have a husband?"

"No," she answered simply.
"Would you like to have one?" I mumbled cautiously.
"Yes," was her unequivocal answer.

With such a clear, unambiguous, and unmistakable answer, a follow-up was blurted out "Could we talk about it?" She agreed and gave me a telephone number.

Two weeks passed while my emotions were evaluated and my intention considered. Surely such a lovely lady was without a man for some good reason. Was she flawed in some way? Was she some religious fanatic? Was she a female iceberg who just didn't like men? Not wanting to give up my newly discovered independence and peace of mind, there was a natural reluctance to marry again.

It was All-Hallows Eve

After the "Do you have a husband?" episode, my objectivity worked patiently for two weeks before her number was dialed. All-Hallows Eve had become Halloween night, a time for children to dress up and go from door to door boldly asking for candy and saying "trick or treat." It was not a romantic night to call a lady, but it was a low risk time. Maybe a conversation opener could be "trick or treat!" She answered, but told me she couldn't talk because her parents were visiting. Was my interest misplaced? Was my assessment of this lady an objective observation or just an emotional wish? Well, that is that, crossed my mind; after all it was Halloween. How could her parents being present make a difference in whether or not she talked with me? Was she under their thumb? Was that the reason she didn't have a man? Such thoughts tumbled through my brain as my next move was pondered. The decision was to give her my telephone number and ask her to call when she had time to talk; thinking... that's the last of that. I will have to find another canoe and another river. "No wonder she's not married!" was the audible outburst of my frustration.

"Who was that on the phone?" Gail's mother asked. "Dr. Hollis Green," she replied. At this her father, the Reverend Henry M. Parks, spoke up with an affirmation: "If Dr. Green is calling Gail, it's O.K., I know him through his books; he is a good man." My phone rang! Who could be calling me on Halloween night?

Gail returned my call and since I was leaving town for several weeks, we arranged to meet for brunch the next day. The rest is history! Well, it is our history, but few know about the facts of this special relationship and marriage.

When I returned from my trip, my heart was pounding with anticipation; I purchased a friendship ring to show my level of interest. We met several times before I had the courage to give her the ring, but nothing prepared me for one little "word" she spoke softly; that one word was "when." During this first serious conversation, she said, "When we get married, I'll be good to you. When we get married, my love will always be true." That one word, "when," has been a key to my happiness these many years. A few months later we decided to get married.

Crucial Relationship Imperative

Before this was to happen, I wanted to get one understanding in place: it is normal for people in a relationship to get upset, but... "***We must never both be upset at the same time***!"

On February 8, 1974, we were married. That simple, but crucial relationship imperative has created a healthy and spiritual marriage. Our history has become His Story as we have worked together in a ministry through education. This companionship and working together included her strengths compensating for my weaknesses in various positions of service: as a pastor, as a professor of education and social change, as Vice-President of a seminary (www.lru.edu). in founding and becoming the first president and chancellor of a graduate school (www.ogs.edu), in establishing a university in Trinidad (www.oasisedu.org), in organizing and operating a publishing business to assist authors with manuscript development and publication (www.globaledadvance.org). Just to remember, with thanksgiving, that providential chance brought us together brings to mind many happy days. Practicing the relationship imperative "***We must never both be upset at the same time!***" has created a cohesiveness that enhances our time together

A Great Mystery

How could one person make such a difference in the life of a man? That is one of the great mysteries of life! That first question began a beautiful friendship that grew into a sweet companionship, and developed into a spiritual fellowship. God is good!

With marriages falling apart all around us, it is good to understand that marriage can work. Provided the relationship has a sound foundation in faith, a clear understanding of roles, solemn agreements with trust, and respect...yes, respect. Consider the meaning of "respect;" it is one key that unlocks the mystery of a good and perpetual marriage relationship.

A Simple Key

Let me share an incident that will explain the true meaning of "respect" and open the door to a better relationship. Eating lunch with friends in a local restaurant, a young man approached:

"Dr. Green, do you ever counsel married couples?"
"Occasionally, I do."
"Could my wife and I come and talk with you?"

The session was arranged and both came, but both seemed somewhat reluctant to speak. I asked them to write down what they wanted the other to change and place it in an envelope. This they did. I opened the wife's envelope and read the list and handed it to the husband. "Read the first one."

"I want him to respect me."
"What does she mean?" I asked.
"I don't have a clue."

Outside the room was a large unabridged dictionary on a stand. "Go look up the word respect," Following my instructions, he returned with a look of consternation, he was asked to share the meaning.

"It means to look at, to pay attention to,..."
"Do you understand what she wants?"
"If you mean, do I understand her statement, 'I want him to respect me.'
"Yes, that is what I mean."
"Yes, I believe I understand the problem; she wants me to look at her and pay attention to her."
"Are you willing to do that?"
"Yes!"

Case closed! Reconciliation began, a child was born; the

family is raising a bright little girl that has become a cohesive force in their relationship. **So another key to happiness in marriage is simply the little word "respect" – to look at, to pay attention to...**

Provided there is shared respect in a relationship, both will receive the attention and appreciation required to maintain a mutual friendship and a workable marriage. Since I have shared the key word "respect" let me go further and say that this little word is the secret to building a "better spouse trap" and the master key needed to make marriage a mutual admiration society.

This book is more than how to find a mate; it is concerned with breaking the cycle of dysfunctional relationships, learning lessons from the past, and guiding the next generation to be more objective and selective in choosing a mate for life. Parents have not completed their work until each child has been nurtured, educated, and guided toward a career and the choice of an appropriate life-mate.

LOVE AND COURTSHIP

During our brief courtship, I sent Gail a small greeting booklet which she kept through the years. Inside the cover, I wrote my understanding of L.O.V.E. in an acrostic: **LOVE IS:**

Learning from the past;
Opening your heart to someone;
Viewing the future with confidence;
Enjoying the present moment.

Through the years we have referred to this acrostic many times to **"improve our conversation and revisit our respect for one another."** The booklet was placed in the tower "Quiet

Time Room" at Oxford Chapel. Hopefully, it will assist others with their Love conversations.

Through the intervening years, especially during my globe trotting to over 100 countries, I have written lyrics and melodies and usually sang them on the telephone to Gail before I arrived home. In response, she would compose prose and read to me. This has been an ongoing experience and has become a tradition worthy of emulation. Excerpts from Love's Extended Conversation are found in the Apendices...it continues and is good!

Hollis L. Green, ThD, PhD
Evergreen Cottage, Lone Mountain
February 8, 2010

Searching for the perfect plan to attract a proper mate?

Chapter One

The Better Spouse Trap

Why the negative term “spouse trap?” The word “trap” was used to get the attention of those looking for a mate. The present system is designed to catch and ensnare a mate, but whether that mate ever becomes a spouse is doubtful. Part of the difficulty with failed marriages is that the participants soon feel trapped in a bad relationship. Why do they feel trapped? When the dating game is over and the spouse that set the trap is tired of the old party time, they want out. They start looking elsewhere for sensual excitement, but there are children and financial obligations that are not easy to evade. The more trapped the individual feels the more their behavior becomes animalistic and violent. The relationship becomes sadistic and abusive and the spouse and children suffer. One more marriage relationship is headed for the dung heap. Another marriage has been sundered. There must be a better way! Why can’t we be more objective in mate selection? How can one avoid being snookered by a smooth talker making a trick shot at the target ball? Probably the best way is to avoid playing snooker!

When one is dating it is easy to walk away. In marriage when the cleaving is hard, the leaving may be even harder. There was a couple where the minister forgot to mail in the signed legal papers after the ceremony. When the husband found out about the problem six months later, he decided since he was not legally married he would just walk away. Adding someone to your life changes your arrangements. The concept of "submit" is to line up under the authority of another. As a single person one is under the authority and guidance of parents. Once married, life must be rearranged, reorganized, reprioritized, and sometimes repaired. Be patient, the right person may come along. It may be similar to catching a butterfly. Do not rush matters, just sit quietly and the butterfly will land on your shoulder. What matters in marriage is that marriage matters. Searching for a proper mate is an important endeavor and worthy of special grace, patience, and perseverance.

A Better Model

In an early effort to learn about the sociology of mate selection, a process no longer in vogue in Jamaica was discovered. In the 1950's a Jamaican cultural model of a non-dating, objective mate-selection plan was used in some circles rather than the current subjective courtship/dating process. The model led to a brokered marriage proposal articulated by the local clergy representing the man. It appeared to be an excellent way for a young man to find a moral mate and begin a mature marriage relationship with the blessing of the church and the bride's family.

A Spin-off

Some socio-historical critics explained the Jamaican model as a spin-off of the arranged marriage system of Europe. It was my understanding the Jamaican effort was fostered by the church to maintain a moral standard among the young and to keep the mate selection process in the objective arena. The process did not deny the erotic dimension, but structured the process to restrain the expression of sexuality until a final choice for a mate was made and the marriage was consummated. It sounded like a better spouse trap to me.

Scheduled to speak at a Jamaican college in 1959, on a Sunday morning after chapel, a member of the faculty invited me to lunch. Not knowing that he was married the evening before and that this was the first Sunday lunch that he and his new bride would share, the invitation was accepted. Had the nature of their relationship been known, the invitation would have been respectfully declined; however, that lunch provided much of the information that was needed to appreciate the Jamaican model of seeking a mate. The advance process was known, but the emotion, the beauty, the grace, the wisdom of the model was demonstrated at the table that Sunday. This is my observation and understanding of how the model worked.

An Overview of the Model

First, an overview of the model would be helpful. It seems that a mature young man ready for marriage would discuss the matter with a local clergyman. The minister would ask him for the names of three young ladies in order of preference: first, second, and third choice. The pastor would then visit each of the young ladies in turn expressing the young man's desire for marriage. If the lady was reluctant to agree, the pastor would explain the advantages of the man: his education, his job or profession, the home he had provided, and the background of his family. If the young lady still refused marriage, the clergyman would go to the next choice and repeat the process. If all three refused marriage, the pastor would then go to the parents of the first choice and explain the advantages of the prospective husband. If the parents were so inclined, they would then discuss the matter with their daughter. If she still resisted marriage to this man, the pastor would go to the parents of the second choice and repeat the process. If necessary the pastor would go to the parents of the third choice. If the process totally failed, the pastor would ask the young man for another list of three choices. When the clergyman finally convinced a young lady and her parents of the marriage, the banns would be posted on the door of the local church to secure input from the community.

During this process, the young man was not allowed to write or speak to either of the young ladies on the list. Only the pastor was allowed to discuss the proposal and the advantages of the marriage. There was no dating, no walks down the lane, or quiet times on the beach. The young man just had to wait for the young lady and her parents to agree, the banns to be posted, and the normal waiting period allowed for others to oppose the marriage for "reason or cause." Instead of a happy and joyful time, the prospective groom passed the time in patient contemplation and some anxious moments when he saw the pastor coming with news that could be good or bad. This did not sound as if it were a good process, but when the after-effects of the wedding were observed at the Sunday lunch it was easy to see the value of the objective model. Both the bride and the groom came to the altar morally ready for marriage without the sexual baggage normally carried in the multiple partner courting and dating process. Sounds like a better spouse trap to me.

Now back to Sunday lunch. It appeared that the husband had a professorship at the local college and had provided a well-furnished home for his new bride. The dining table was a long refectory-type fixture with short ends and long sides. The benches on each side would accommodate several children with chairs at each end for the parents. Upon entering the dining room it became apparent that the new bride had made a special meal and special seating arrangements. As the guest, I was seated on one of the long benches on the side of the table while the chairs at both ends had been moved to one end. The bride and groom were to be seated on the small end of the table. It was at that end of the refectory-type table that the real benefit of the Jamaican model of arranging marriage was observed.

A Sensual Episode

With no dating experience and only a short time from the Saturday evening wedding to the Sunday lunch that included attendance at the Sunday morning service and the invitation of a lunch guest, the lack of familiarity with each other physically caused each touch and each glance to become a sensual episode. The smiles, giggles, and even overt laughter were obvious. It seemed that each body movement and each word were received as a sensual signal that at last we are together with the blessing of family, church, and community. It sure sounded like a better spouse trap to me.

Five Decades Later

It is now five decades since this episode and things have changed in Jamaica and around the world. Romantic love and serial dating have replaced most of the working arrangements that for generations brought couples together with the guidance of mature parents and enabled them to launch a stable marriage relationship in which they could build a family. Divorce has intruded on the sanctity of marriage and dysfunctional relationships have replaced the vows with violence. The children and the community both suffer from the obvious changes in the mate-selection process and the nature of the dysfunctional relationship. The young still need a working model of mate selection that is objective. Someone must build a better spouse trap.

The Mating Game

An old proverb described the mating game as "A boy chases a girl until she catches him." This process was both positive and negative. A simple word in common Greek described both sides of this issue. The word *zogreo* put two constructs together meaning "to take alive or make a prisoner of" and was used symbolically "to capture or ensnare another." The word could easily describe the age old battle of the sexes where one or both became a hostage in the conflict of sensual attraction.

To Catch Alive

A clear picture of this construct may be learned from the sacred writings of Luke and Paul. In the Greek New Testament the word is used only twice; once to tell Peter that his future would be to **"catch men alive"** to advance the will of God (Luke 5:10), and Paul uses the word in a similar sense to describe a man captured alive and freed from the trap of the devil.

22. Flee youthful passions: but pursue righteousness, faith, love, peace with the ones calling on the Lord out of a clean heart. 23. But foolish and ignorant questions avoid, knowing they breed nothing but arguments. 24. And the servant of the Lord must not struggle with arguments; but behave kindly toward all men, teaching appropriately with unwearied tolerance, 25. Understanding those who oppose in order to instruct properly; if perhaps God will change their mind to acknowledge the truth; 26.Having been **captured** by the will of God they may remove themselves from **the trap** of the devil. (2 Timothy 2:22-26 DNT)

Men Caught in a Trap

St. Paul wrote to young Timothy that there were intoxicated men caught in a trap to do the devil's work but who could be awakened by spiritual forces and could free themselves for a positive future. The clear implication is that these men were under the influence of bad company and somewhat intoxicated perhaps by some stupefying potion and caught in a snare or net but could be rescued from this perilous condition by their own positive efforts aided by divine guidance. What was the lesson young Timothy learned as an unmarried man? He must seek non-sexual friendships and be cautious about becoming ensnared in Satan's relational game of sensual infatuation. He also learned that there were spiritual strengths available to assist him in the process of relationship building.

The Other Side of the Issue

In Luke's gospel, it seems that Peter and other fishermen had toiled all night and caught nothing, but when they followed a simple plan to "look at the other side of the issue," they were successful. The Master Teacher told Peter, "Do not fear the future; you will be able to catch men alive to advance the cause using this simple plan." Catching a fish alive or in this case capturing a man alive meant that the fish and the man were useful and usable for the purpose for which they were captured. It was clear that the effort could be positive. What was the big lesson in Luke? Fish were taken to be devoured, but the man was to be "taken alive" for devotion, attachment, and fidelity related to a positive future. Since Luke's gospel tells "all that Christ began to do and teach," can we not see a lesson here for developing positive relationships?

Jesus gave a poor fisher of fish a simple plan to work without fear to win men for a good cause. Could this be an easy plan for constructive relationships "to have a friend one must be friendly without a hidden agenda?" Could mate-selection be as uncomplicated as looking at the other side of the issue (forgetting the sensual and simply seeking a platonic-friendship) so the courting and conniving become unnecessary to achieve the positive goal of finding a proper mate for marriage?

Attracted to Surface Charm

Often to be absorbed in the dating game is to be attracted

to surface charm and physical beauty without giving notice to the negative qualities that could have harmful influence on a long-term relationship. Without a clear understanding of the possibility of non-sexual platonic-friendships, dating partners become fascinated with personality rather than character qualities and develop an intense but short-lived and irrational passion, rather than genuine affection. It is easy to become preoccupied with living for the moment rather than considering the problems of a long-term relationship. Sadly the true loveliness and genuine worth and value of a potential marriage partner cannot be objectively assessed in the heat of passion. Infatuation is not a proper basis for marriage. Remember, beauty is only skin deep, but spitefulness, malice, and ugly attitude go all the way to the bone and overflows into the relationship.

Primarily Platonic

The early stage of a relationship should be primarily platonic without the baggage of sensuality. In the modern sense, platonic love is a non-sexual affectionate relationship. It should be chaste but passionate. This is a time to learn about a future mate without the distracting elements of sexuality and permit their wisdom and beauty to inspire the mind and soul in the direction of a long-term relationship. The issue of procreation must not complicate and obligate the early stage of a relationship. It is wiser for sexual expression to be redirected into the intellectual and emotional spheres. This may seem paradoxical in the light of the current dating game process, but it is a way to avoid the hazards that destroy many relationships. The Jamaican model of mate- selection deals with these dynamics and is explained in the next chapter.

Without Strings or Rings

Some are addicted to the "rush" that comes with a new relationship. What they really want is a connection without strings or rings. They get high on sweaty palms and flushed skin, characteristic of falling in love. These are caused by a rush of brain chemicals similar to amphetamines. As the body gets used to these chemicals, it takes more of them to maintain the rush that some crave. Without this they seek for another partner that will supply the rush. Some have suggested that this may explain why some people jump from one relationship to another. They crave the rush of falling in love and are addicted to the attraction phase of a new relationship. Without growth and maturity they are doomed to repeat the process and break more and more hearts in the cycle.

Distinctive Differences

Complete togetherness is not possible. A couple in a relationship remain separate individuals with all their distinctive differences. Each one must be allowed to remain dissimilar and grow at his/her own pace. Such differences will cause tension and discomfort. It requires hard work to keep a healthy relationship together. No two living things are exactly the same, not even identical twins. There must be spaces in the togetherness just as there must be rests in music or one cannot hear the rhythm or the harmony.

Familiarity may Breed Contempt

Each must share their hearts, but retain control of their own heart strings. A couple must stand together, but not too close. They are pillars of a special Temple and must have a certain distance to provide support for the relationship. Remember, certain trees cannot grow in each other's shadow. No one is perfect and when a couple gets too close they learn things about the other they did not need to know. The connectedness of marriage may be able to handle the knowledge of negative details. Evidence exists in one's physical body of the significant connection with their birth mother prior to their life outside the womb. One cannot avoid various levels of connectedness. If one gets too close or moves too far away from a significant other, there will be a change in the relationship. Either the heart grows fonder or the heart grows cold.

Unconditional Love

A healthy relationship requires unconditional love and mutual commitment. Love overlooks human mistakes, but sees clearly the pattern of action and reaction that affects the maturity of a relationship. Forgiveness means not to hold something against another in the future. Individual acts which violate the integrity of a relationship may be forgiven, but patterns of unhealthy behavior must be confronted honestly. This does not mean that one accepts wrongdoing in a partner without dealing with the consequences and the patterns. Areas of concern must be addressed and unhealthy behavior modified to maintain an equitable relationship.

Personal Integrity in Dating

The foundation stone of a healthy relationship is personal integrity. One must not only see the ideal to which they aspire, the reality of personal flaws must be acknowledged, cataloged and maturely handled to construct an adequate self-worth and to insure personal integrity. Dating is in fact an adventure of being ordinary. It is only fair to show the real you so others may make an informed judgment about a relationship. It is also fair-minded to expect the same from a dating partner. There is a profound difference in dating and marriage. In the dating game either individual may call time out or walk away without major consequences; however, in marriage commitment, trustworthiness, and loyalty create a relationship that is more secure and much harder to break. There is no just walking away or going home to mama!

Pledge to Fidelity in Marriage

The marriage commitment includes a pledge to fidelity. There is to be no disloyalty, falseness, or betrayal in a marriage relationship. Whether or not your spouse is your soul mate, your spouse must be your sole mate as long as the marriage contract is in force. A stable marriage requires an exclusive relationship without deceitfulness and objective negotiated settlements to all relational problems or disagreements. A marriage commitment is more binding than an appointment for a date. One cannot just up and cancel a marriage. Dating is an informal arrangement with no strings while marriage is a legal contract binding under law and based on the integrity and fidelity of both parties.

Mate Selection

The possibility of mate-selection is the reason dating is important; it provides the data to assist with making the decision to form a permanent union. Yes, permanent unless broken by outside influence. All difficulties should be settled within the confines of the marriage without bringing others into the mix. Mature human beings who have deep affection for each other should be able to work through their difficulties and solve the problems that normally arise in a marriage. It is the unexpected or third-party problems that confuse the issue. This is why mate-selection is important. Through observation an objective decision based on honest criteria should determine life-mate selection.

Like a fish on a hook,
I was caught in the dating trap!

Chapter Two

The Basics Of Mate Selection

Strong Views

My mother was a young but a tough one-room grammar school teacher and later a dean in a nursing school and retired as a college dean of women. She had strong views on dating, mate selection, marriage, raising children, and building relationships. During WW II my older sister wrote a soldier encouraging letters for four years about home and family. Mother's instruction was "Don't put any baloney in your letters. That boy is over there fighting for his country and doesn't need to be distracted by romance." Overseas letters would come and my sister would rush home and ask, "Did I get any mail today?"

On one occasion, a letter came and my younger sister put it in the old ice box where the melting ice blurred the ink. My sister was furious and complained to mother. When the child was asked why she put the letter in the ice box, the answer was revealing. "I put it in the ice box to keep the baloney from spoiling." After writing a soldier for four years, my sister ended up marrying a sailor, a cousin of a friend. She knew him only a few weeks, but the marriage has lasted over 60 years and produced four of the finest children, two boys and two girls, and now many grandchildren and a few great grandchildren. What is the moral of this story? Long term dating may not find the proper mate, but when one finds that significant other, the heart knows! Normally, infatuation is short-lived while love can last a life time.

Mother's Dating Rules

Good manners are like traffic rules for a relationship. There are no minimum or maximum speed limits on the road to good relationships, just a few rules to keep a couple on the straight and narrow path. Persistence is required to achieve excellence and quality of relationships will be tested over time. Mother's first rule of dating was "Remain objective! And fall in love intelligently and not too fast." The second rule was "Never date anyone you would not want to marry, and if you discover some flaw in the person during the early stage of a relationship, stop seeing them immediately." Her third rule was "Be careful not to fall in love with love; it may be only infatuation (an intense but short-lived and irrational passion), and be sure you are in love with the person." And finally for those mature enough to marry she had a final rule, "Once you have objectively evaluated the entire situation and decided to get married... get married! Long engagements create problems for moral people. The struggle with emotions and passion can have a negative result on a long-term relationship."

Love and Sympathy

A postscript to her rules was advice for those who during the engagement period discovered a flaw, defect, blemish, or imperfection with which they did not wish to live the rest of their life: "Break off the engagement immediately." If she were asked why make such a drastic decision, she would explain that love and sympathy are close together and are not easily separated. This causes individuals to continue with wedding plans out of sympathy because they do not want to hurt a friend. This makes for a negative start and a central rule in philosophy has a powerful and dramatic effect on this situation: "One can never reach a positive conclusion beginning with a negative premise." And then she would say, "What part of 'never' do you not understand?"

Child-adult Dichotomy

What is the difference in a relationship strategy in a child-adult dichotomy? It has been suggested that one should court the adult, but should marry the child. While objectively observing the adult and subjectively seeing the child, one obtains a more comprehensive perspective of the person. During the dating phase of a relationship one should see a fully developed grown-up with normal levels of maturity. Dating is not just fun and games; it is serious business that relates to the quality of one's future. However, when an adult is watched attentively, one will notice their sense of humor and the innocent child-like qualities. It is this formal/informal observation that permits the unwritten criteria to function.

Court the Adult, Marry the Child

Dating is similar to the soup of the day. A young man asked the waitress, "How is the soup de jour?" Her answer, "I don't know, but it must be good.; we have it every day." The innate criteria for mate-selection have not been fully articulated, but it must be good - it is used over and over again. Perhaps boys observe the physical features of females in their family and girls do the opposite. In this way they come up with unwritten criteria of how a potential mate should appear and behave. Support for this theory comes from observation of the choices made for a second mate after the death of a spouse. The choice often favors the first spouse in general appearance and in the cases where this is a fact, this innate criteria theory is supported.

My wife's name is "Gloria Gail." As a professional, I dated "Gloria," but married "Gail." Business colleagues called her Gloria at work, but Gail is the name her family still uses. Even her grand nieces call her Aunt Gail when she gets down in the floor to play games or when she has a fancy "tea party" for one of the little nieces of the family. Yes, I am married to Gail, but Gloria and I work together in a home-based business during retirement. How is that for an adult/child dichotomy?

A Safe Mode

Adults work; children play. However, when one marries the "child" they are seeking an innocent, growing, developing person who will become exactly what one desires in a mate. When they date the "child" and marry the "adult" they are disappointed because the adult wants to settle down. This unrealistic predicament creates difficulties in the marriage relationship. Adults form friendly associations and interact on a mature level and connect with others at a cognitive level. Children engage in enjoyable activities, play games, develop friendly competition, connect with other at the affective level, and generally deal with situations in a "safe-mode setting." Children often portray different characters and make various impressions on others and in the process have fun.

Stereotyped

Adults are themselves behaving in a stereotyped manner and are categorized by others according to an oversimplified standardized image. Adults are burdened with duties or activities that are part of an occupation and are identified by their work or profession: she is an administrator, he is a counselor; she is a nurse, he is a physician.

Baby Talk

Dating should be a mature process, but marriage gives opportunity to enjoy the innocence of childhood in a safe arena. Have you noticed that mature adults talk to their spouse in "baby talk" and use made-up words to describe events, episodes, and even body parts? The interactions of married folk are often childish and juvenile and are conducted in a playful manner when they are alone. Married folk have dual *modus operandi*: one protocol for the public and one code of behavior for their personal and private time together. Learn the act of giving and receiving. Love takes time. It needs a history of giving and receiving, laughing and crying.

Listening is a Key to Marriage

Not only in the early stages of a relationship but also throughout the marriage, listening skills are necessary to assure a more perfect union. The issue is not hearing, but listening. Three levels of hearing relate to human communication. The first level is the level of non-hearing "having ears and hear not;" in other words, the ear hears the sounds but ignores it. A second level of hearing is the ability to hear the words, record them in a special part of the brain and even recall the exact words but never obtain the understanding of their meaning. This is a kind of recording/playback device that is often used to avoid the content of the conversation. Sometimes it is hearing the general idea of the conversation and concentrating on a reply or rebuttal rather that listening to the whole story.

Analysis and Action

The final level is listening. This requires both analysis and action. When one gives attention to the spoken word, listens to the sounds, and understands the meaning — this is listening. This requires one to examine the words in detail in order to better understand or draw conclusions. When such an analysis takes place, normally some kind of action or response is forthcoming. Listening by both parties is necessary for progress in relationship development.

Listening says, "Come closer, touch my heart and my mind." It has been noted that "listening is the highest form of touching absent physical contact." (See Appendix B "You Touch Me") Listening has also been associated with a replacement for or a precursor to sexual intimacy. This may explain the behavior of some individuals who partially listen but prefer to go directly to some form of sexual contact. This may explain the root of sexual abuse by family members, but it is not to excuse such behavior.

Language of the Heart

Learn to speak the language of the heart. Note that h-**ear**-t contains an "ear" this is the "ear" with which one listens attentively to the words of a marriage partner. This is good because a marriage mate has many "unspoken words" that must be h**ear**d with the h**ear**t and clearly understood. Dynamic listening is active, vigorous, energetic, and is always focused on your partner. Active listening encourages both parties of the marriage relationship to listen with attention and stick to the task at hand in spite of all distractions. When your partner feels that you are listening they will be more apt to attend with interest to what you have to say when it becomes your turn. Use the 30-second rule, that is, wait at least 30 seconds until you are certain your partner has adequately expressed the pertinent concern. During that 30 second wait meditate on this prayer: **Lord help me remember that nothing will happen to me today that you and I together can't handle!** Without this pause one cannot make an informed response. The one-half minute of silence prevents an emotional response and provides time to think about what was said and respond intelligently. Real communication requires listening and receiving on the part of both parties to the conversation.

The Seven C's of Marital Listening

Do not confuse hearing and listening. Hearing is the physical aspect of perceiving sound. Listening is analyzing and understanding the sound. It is hearing with a purpose. Basic listening skills: concentration, consideration, contemplation, comportment, compliment, celebration, and commemoration are called the Seven C's of marital listening.

1. **Concentration** permits one to be attentive to the words being spoken and become absorbed in the meaning of the words. This enables immediate thinking of how to apply and relate the meaning to the general discussion.
2. **Consideration** is to add value to the words heard, reflect on this value by reproducing the concepts in one's own words, and deliberately attributing value to the conversation.
3. **Contemplation** is mulling over the significance of the words and the worth, importance, and usefulness of the discussion.
4. **Comportment** is the overall behavior of the listener and a general assessment that answers the question: "Do the words match the conduct and character exhibited?" This is the final effort to add credibility to the discussion. The more the listener values the speaker; the greater the significance of the words spoken.
5. **Compliment** is the listener expressing approval of the remarks of a valued speaker.
6. **Celebration** is a positive and pleasant response to good news.
7. **Commemoration** is the act of honoring the speaker for what they say and where they stand.

Poor Listeners

When a partner's words are valued; listening is both easy and rewarding. Most individuals tend to be poor listeners; this is particularly true of the selfish who seek only a sexual encounter. How well a partner listens is a major factor in building long-term relationships. One listens to obtain information, to better understand another person, and to learn important facts not yet in evidence in the conversation.

Clearly the improvement of listening skills should be a regular part of relationship building. Good listening skills will also prevent conflict and misunderstandings. Everyone will benefit when listening skills are improved.

Improve Listening Skills

Maintain eye contact with the person talking. Face-to-face contact keeps one focused on the task at hand and keeps both parties involved. Focus on content by listening to every word. Forget about the faulty memory or halting speech; just concentrate on the words and their true meaning. Avoid personal or emotional reaction to anything said. At times one hears what they want to hear and not what is actually said. Remain objective and open-minded. Do not permit distractions to cause your mind to wander. Avoid anything that disturbs your concentration or what is being said. Make certain you are as comfortable as the location and situation permits. Listening is not a passive act. You must concentrate on what is said in order to process the information and use it to benefit the relationship. Maintain an active role in the conversation or be a good silent listener if that is appropriate. Use any gap in the rate of speech to assimilate the words. Always keep your focus on the person talking. Practice good listening skills and your listening will improve.

Even Those Unspoken

There are several ways to improve listening skills. Be deliberate with your listening and response and constantly remind yourself that your objective is to truly hear what is being said, even the unspoken stuff. In my home is a framed cross-stitch with the words: "Called to listen to the needs of others, even those unspoken." The keepsake came from my father-in-law's study. He was a pastor, but the words are appropriate to everyone, especially a married couple. Body language is important to understanding a conversation. Then there is the adage, "What you are speaks so loudly I can't hear what you say!" Improve your listening, it is worth the effort.

Attend with interest to what is being said. Give your undivided attention. Do not waste time, it is precious. Do not be distracted by thinking about a rebuttal when you should be listening, you will miss something important. Do not permit yourself to have side conversations when you should be listening.

Demonstrate that you are listening. Smile and nod and use other facial expressions to let the person know you are listening. Small verbal comments such as yes, uh huh, may encourage the person to speak more frankly.

Offer constructive comments. Do not let your own assumptions or beliefs distort what is being said. Listeners are first required to understand what is being said. Disagreement or questions come later. When the opportunity is presented or there is a time for questions, be kind and paraphrase by saying, "What I heard..." "Did you say...?" "Is this what you mean...?"

Avoid premature conclusions. Do not interrupt when someone is speaking. It frustrates you and it totally irritates others because they think you are not listening. It is usually best to wait for a logical opening to express yourself. Remember the 30-second rule.

Provide a measured response. If you know the facts to be wrong or the person expressed a lack of understanding of the data in the records, clarify the information in a constructive tone. Be candid, open and honest in all responses.

A Failure to Listen

A failure to listen is insulting and equivalent to a social snub. Marriage partners are particularly susceptible to this feeling. When a partner senses that the other is not listening, he/

she feels defenseless and exposed to dangers seen and unseen. Listening then becomes a form of protection and a show of affection that is deeply appreciated by a marriage partner. Practice dynamic listening in at-risk situations. If the marriage has children be especially careful when dividing your time between or among children and your spouse, but you must never divide your love. Two good ears, two focused eyes and two minutes of your time may be the best solution to relationship problems. Time is often a great healer and a kind of ministry of presence. In fact the best way to spell love is “t-i-m-e.”

Chapter Three

The Match-Making Business

Appropriate for a Bride

Should one consider the cost of divorce, the million-dollar question becomes obvious: "Is God still in the match-making business?" God no longer takes a rib from a sleeping man and makes a woman who is appropriate for a bride. Even though sacred writings declared that finding a wife was a good thing. Scripture did not say the relationship was made in heaven or that it would be perfect. When Adam complained "the woman you gave me" and Eve made excuses for her behavior and declared "The serpent mesmerized me," deception and disobedience entered the garden relationship. Perhaps this is when God went out of the match-making business. No one, not even God, wants to hear complaining and excuse making.

Calamity Jane Character Flaw

Since God's chosen companion for Adam had a kind of Calamity Jane character flaw and brought humiliating embarrassment to Adam and the human race, what is man's prospect of finding a loving and supportive companion? Even when God placed a sinless man and an unspoiled woman together in a beautiful garden, with no debts and no credit cards, there was discord. They were not gods, but mere human beings. The present generation may ask, "Who was Calamity Jane and what relevance does this have with Eve?" It may be a stretch, but Jane was a frontier woman who scouted for the army. Although she had a good side and exhibited kindness and compassion towards the sick and needy, she was an alcoholic who traded sexual favors for personal gain. Likewise, Eve made decisions for personal gain.

Down a Primrose Path

Eve was clothed in innocence, but was seduced by what appeared to be a harmless conversation that included a half-truth which was in fact a whole lie. She was promised a better life than being the partner of a garden keeper. Did Eve have an unfulfilled desire for carnal knowledge? Is this why she was deceived by the idea of becoming wise? She was led down a primrose path to see things never seen before. She was told it would be a pleasant journey and she would become the wiser. Eve's dysfunction was more than a wardrobe malfunction of her innocence and Adam's failure to obey God's rules was more than weakness surrendered to Eve's will; it was blatant disobedience. Eve was misinformed, but Adam was hoodwinked into behavior that displeased God.

Male and Female Reproduction

The problem of Adam and Eve was not some physical act. The concept of male and female reproduction was included in the plant and animal life before Adam was made. All things were made male and female and Adam was made "male" before Eve was made "female." All creation was under the command to be "fruitful and fill the earth." God created the concept of sexual intercourse even before Eve was made. Consequently, the fall of Adam and Eve was not caused by sexual activity. It was acts of disobedience to God's direct command. Adam and Eve clearly understood the prescribed limitations of their behavior and acted with disregard of this knowledge.

Ahead of God's Timing

It should be noted that sex does not improve a relationship; in fact, sexual activity changes one's perspective on the relationship. In counseling a man who wanted a long engagement for what appeared to be personal and selfish reasons, it was assumed that sexual activity had already begun. There was no rush to marry because he had what he wanted (unless something better came along in the meantime). To clearly get the message across, the man was told if you want the "milk" you must buy the whole cow. One must remember that **marriage is not only finding someone with whom to live out the rest of your life**, but **marriage is finding someone you cannot live without for the rest of your life**.

If not sex, then what was the sin in the garden? Where did the "apple stuff" originate? The tradition could have come from the Latin *malam* (apple) which was similar to the Latin *malum* (evil). Regardless of what the garden variety of sin actually was, if one chooses to make it sexual then perhaps even though God had planned the concept of reproduction, Adam and Eve may have jumped ahead of God's timing. Sex does not make things better; it makes things different. Perhaps God wanted Adam's work in the garden planning for the care and safety of plants and animals and his wife before children came that would take away his time from the first task. Perhaps this is where the "timing issue" enters the debate about when sexual activity should begin. Regardless, of exactly what this unspecified act was, the cause was deception and disobedience and there were consequences for the failure to follow the rules. This is a lesson that most have not learned.

Shakespeare Wrote

Shakespeare wrote in Hamlet (Act 1, Scene III) of the primrose path in relation to one who had little moral restraint, or sought the easy and pleasurable path, or those folk who would not listen to their own advice. Shakespeare suggested that some had strong guidelines for others, but did not follow their own rules. He was concerned about the behavior of parents and moral prophets who became "good bad examples" to the young. It appears that Shakespeare understood the human element that intrudes, interferes, and interrupts all human communication and relationships. Since his writings are studied by most students, hopefully some will finally learn the lesson that promiscuity and "bad examples" complicate the human equation as one faces life with the opposite sex. What is that lesson: "that two expressions divided by an equal sign are of the same value." The truth is clear when examples of undiscriminating sexual behavior become known there is little restraint for the young. It is simply "monkey see; monkey do" and it becomes open season for sowing wild oats which ultimately harms the marriage relationship. Research supports a relationship between the number of pre-marital sexual encounters and post-marriage unfaithfulness.

Serious Human Endeavor

Mate selection is a serious human endeavor. Presently it appears that the constructs of dating and mating sound similar, but are grossly different. Dating has become a search for sexual mating. Mate selecting is altogether a different story. The qualifying questions in the dating game are (1) Are you seeking a willing accomplice in sex, or (2) are you searching for a lifelong mate for wedlock? In the simplest of terms, dating must be more than a scavenger hunt for the lowest common denominator sexual partner; it should be a serious journey to find two compatible people who belong together who can be more than friends and can establish a long-term intimate and exclusive relationship. Surely, spiritual guidance can assist with the process, but the burden is on the individuals involved. Religion is not the "bogeyman" here; moral decency and the future happiness in marriage are at stake.

Flawed Judgment

Divine providence entrusts the foreboding task of selecting a life-mate to the flawed judgment of an emotional human choice. For this reason couples should seek advice from family and friends, because it is difficult to remain objective in the process of mate selection. One needs rules to follow and boundaries to contain the process. It is similar to sheep that must have either a shepherd or a fence to keep them from going astray. In the dating game both are needed.

A Clinical Element

Choosing a mate is a gigantic responsibility and is critical business with a clinical element. Why use the words business and clinical in relationship to marriage? Because a business venture has a risk factor and risk should be noted in a marriage commitment. The clinical aspect of mate selection has to do with experimental elements and the need for dispassionate objectivity. Since about one-half of all marriages fail and nearly three-fourths of second marriages do not last, all participants must be cautious. This places the mate selector on a treadmill, which is a monotonous and seemingly endless task. The journey has hazards, pitfalls, dangers, and perils and requires precaution, wisdom in sifting through events determined by chance. However, a good marriage relationship is worth the time and the effort required to fall in love intelligently, to choose objectively and cautiously, to marry with honor, and to do adequate relationship maintenance to make marriage work.

Two Becoming One Flesh

When two walk together in the lighted pathway that shines

from spiritual guidance, their agreement and partnership with Providence will enhance their relationship with each other and provide guidance for problem solving and the nurturing of children. This may sound a little cliché because some feel that religion has lost its original effectiveness or power from overuse, but a personal intimacy with a divine source of guidance can be a reality. Sexual activity between a married couple certainly assists with the bonding of the relationship, but sex alone does not bind them to a single purpose. Most people are fully aware that marriage or sexual intercourse does not change two people into one person, it is clear that the couple remains two distinct individuals. The intimate nature of sexual expression may bring a couple closer emotionally, but it may also alienate a person based on a bad experience.

A relative is one connected by marriage contract or blood. A blood relative is a person related by birth. Individuals who have the same gene pool are kinfolk and are a part of ones larger or extended family. Sacred writings deal with both the connection by contract in marriage and the relationship by birth. Husband and wife are not blood related; they have a contract arrangement where they agree to function within certain parameters. In the process of developing a cherished intimacy, the sexual function becomes a natural expression. This sexual expression may only meet a physical need, but it should demonstrate both affection and desire for each other and may also produce a conception from which a new body, a new living person is formed.

Long-term Results

The Hebrew language makes clear that two becoming "one flesh" does not directly relate to the brief sexual encounter, but defines the long-term results of an extended sexual experience. The results are the combining of two gene pools into the formation of a new body, a real person; that is the first child. The Hebrew word (basar) means flesh, body, living creature, or blood relation. The Hebrew word used in Genesis 2:7 for "soul" (nephesh) was used for "life" in Leviticus 17:11 "The life (nephesh) of the flesh (basar) is in the blood." The word for flesh (basar) is the same as Genesis 3:24 for one flesh. It appears that Genesis 3:24 "Therefore shall a man leave his father and his mother, and shall cleave unto his wife: and they shall be one flesh (basar)," clearly indicates that regardless of other possible occurrence or result, the marriage relationship will in time produce a new body, a real person, a blood relation to both mother and father.

The Same Results

This argument is further supported by the New Testament (Matthew 19:5,6; 1 Corinthians 6:16) where the word "twain or two" may be translated "both" shall become one (first) "flesh" (body or human being). This is where the male and the female "both" become one flesh. Even if the traditional understanding is sexual intercourse, the results are the same: a new life, a new human being is a consequence of the sexual encounter. Mother and father and then blood-related through the combined gene pool in the child. In conception the blood is furnished by the father's sperm and the mother's egg nourishes the unborn offspring in the womb until birth. This produces the new life which is a combination of the gene pools of the parents; thus, they are both apart of one new life. Sexual expression then has a long-term result in building the family. Casual or indiscriminate sexual encounters appear to violate the Creator's long-term reason for dividing the human race into male and female. The clear injunction was "Be fruitful and fill the earth!" God did not approve of the "one night stand." Divine approval is for the long-term commitment that produces a family.

The Central Point

In the New Testament "where two or three are gathered

together" (Matthew 18:20), there is a divine presence in the middle of the couple. This suggests that a couple may have a divine presence as the central point of their relationship and when the first child is born (a blood-relation), the child is brought into the fellowship of the divine presence as a third member of the family. As children are born into the family, they are added to the mix. This verse is clear that the divine source can be in the "midst" or center/middle of the family. This is the way to construct a family that sticks together. Perhaps the old adage is true: "The family who pray together stays together."

A Usable Resource

This reminds me of a story about a couple and their young son on top of a mountain and the child asked, "How far does God's love reach?" The father patiently pointed north, south, east, and west and said, "God's love reaches as far as you can see in all directions." The child responded, "Then we are right in the middle of God's love." That is the idea of marriage and family cohesiveness. It is a spiritual bond that binds a couple and a family together. When a couple or family realizes that the power of the divine is available for the asking, they are empowered with a usable resource.

Self-examination

The first step is self-examination. What kind of mate do you need to permit his/her strengths to support your weaknesses? What can I bring to a relationship? Yes, "relationship;" it is a connection, a bond, a liaison, attachment, friendship, fraternity, a participation, and a fellowship. This fellowship must not be a battleship, but a two-person canoe with two oars on an easy flowing stream. The canoe must not drift, but always be pointed upstream with both occupants rowing at an easy pace. If only one rows, the canoe will go in circles. Should neither row, the canoe will drift downstream toward the fast-moving white water or the waterfall. Forward progress requires a team effort. Both occupants must row together.

Awareness

A sense of awareness develops that they live and function in the center of divine grace. This however does not mean that saying a simple prayer or reciting a devotional program is going to completely smooth out the journey, but it will better prepare the participants to deal with the problems along the way. There is also a prohibition that once a couple is joined together in matrimony all the saints, sinners, and the whole society should work together to make the union wholesome and productive. The warning is also clear, "Let no man put asunder."

There is nothing wrong with being single, yet God said, "It is not good for man to be alone." And Paul wrote in consideration of the times and the difficulties of relationships perhaps one should choose to remain alone rather than risk an unequal yoke that could produce bad days and worse nights. He made it clear that for the sake of moral behavior should one be tempted by irrepressible desires or if a couple could not contain their passion, they should marry (1 Corinthians 7: 1-21). The contemporary youth would say, "Get a room!" However, the better plan would be if the attraction is this strong, plan a marriage. If you do not wish to arrange marriage, remember that someday this person will be another person's spouse. Do you have the right to violate that future?

The Infallibility Syndrome

A religious friend who was sundered said, "When one feels that a marriage was made in heaven, blessed by the church, supported by the family, and the couple seems to love each other deeply, it was easy to develop an infallibility syndrome. That is, that nothing can or will go wrong; that God will keep us together. I assumed that my marriage was a self-sustaining venture. The marriage ceremony including about meeting in the presence of God and the prayer was that the Holy Trinity would bless, preserve and keep us together till death. The ceremony included "What God has joined together let no man put asunder." Therefore, it was assumed that God was going to do any required maintenance to keep the marriage together. This is why my marriage failed and we were sundered. That word "asunder" is an old term meaning "(1) in a sundered or divided state; in different directions; apart; separately; (2) into parts or pieces, as in an explosion." That is what happened! Because my concept of infallibility, I believed my marriage was perfect, watertight, and incapable of being sundered, until the explosion came!"

A Partnership

Parents are obligated to freely provide their children with whatever they need to grow and develop into a mature and productive adult. However, the obligations of a marriage partner do not include being the "parent" of a partner or providing everything a partner needs or wants freely. Marriage is a partnership and a joint venture where both must bring to the table those building blocks required to sustain a relationship. These building blocks are supposed to remain available for use on the table throughout the marriage.

Each partner has qualities that should complement the other. This brings balance and creates agreement and a pleasing combination to avoid human discord that could make a relationship unpleasant. In selecting a partner for marriage one must determine if there is sufficient common ground to support going the distance "till death us do part."

A Genitive Team Effort

Marriage is not a thirty-year mortgage or a five-year car note or a two-year honeymoon. It is much more! Marriage is an investment of time and energy in relationship and building a family. Marriage and family are constructed systematically and have a genitive relationship or a sense of belonging. A construct state in Hebrew and Semitic languages from which many concepts about marriage and relationships are obtained is a form where a noun is followed by a noun that has a genitive relationship to it. In English grammar nouns, pronouns, and objectives that indicate possession or a sense of belonging are in the genitive case. This means marriage is a genitive team effort that includes the parents and children living and working together in harmony in a single domicile with one central purpose: to move forward together.

It is this sense of belonging that forms the force that holds families together through both good and bad times. Of course there are exceptions, and exceptions are forms of excuses. Perhaps my mother's definition of excuse would shed light on this subject: "An excuse is the skin off a reason stuffed with a lie." There are always exceptions and excuses in human relationships otherwise there would be nothing for human beings to grumble and complain about. The human element is a dominate aspect of married life. No amount of religious consecration will change the fact that a married couple is made up of two human beings.

Sad expressions of what happened on the way to the altar!

Like a mouse,
I escaped the pussy cat, but was caught in a baited trap.

Like a bear seeking food,
I was caught in a hunter's trap.

Like a lion on the prowl,
I fell in a poacher's pit.

Like a lost calf,
I was captured by rustlers.

www. trap.com/online.dating/find.a.mate/games/

Chapter Four

The Human Element

Get it Right the First Time

The human element is one of the controlling elements that must be factored into the marriage relationship. In the culture of the romantic system of mate selection about one-half of all first marriages fail. It is even worse for second marriages. Why can't we get it right the first time by fostering a sensible mate-selection process that the young find reasonable and practical? Remember the old adage, "An ounce of prevention is worth a pound of cure?" When will we initiate a remedial assistance system for dysfunctional relationships that salvages the marriages worth saving and enables the orderly dissolution of others with the least disadvantage to the children and society? How can society find an equitable way to care for and support the disadvantaged children from these failed relationships and avoid continued abuse and abandonment? Why not enforce a compulsory child support compensation process against those who choose to abandon responsibility for biological children? This would make parents accountable for sexual behavior. It would also enable others to care for these abandoned offspring more easily. No exceptions. No excuses!

Little Value for Human Life

The young must be taught the seriousness of bringing a new life into the world. Why do the young date and mate, become sexually promiscuous, produce a child and bring the unwanted offspring home for mother or grandmother to care for as if it were a lost puppy or an unwanted parakeet? Why does this happen? Likewise, in this age of quick abortion why is there so little value for human life? Is there no sense of responsibility or concern for protecting human life? What could be the antecedent cause that produced such behavior? Could parents be complicit in this phenomenon?

Poor Training with Pets

Parents are responsible for the training the next generation. Children are given pets and should be taught to care for living things but are allowed to play with them but are not taught the responsibility for or held accountable for their care. Most parents give their children household pets such as gold fish, hamsters, puppies, kittens, and birds. With childlike sincerity the children promise to feed and clean up after, and generally care for the pet. When they fail at this task, rather than using it as a lesson about caring for life, parents normally do the dirty work and give the children a pass in the area of care and responsibility. Could this be a partial explanation as to why teens abort an unwanted pregnancy or put an out of wedlock child up for adoption or abandon their offspring to the care of mother or grandmother? Children learn from the failure of parents to use each opportunity to teach the value of life. They assume they can play, have fun and someone else will pay the bill and pick up the pieces.

No Sense of Accountability

When the dating games start, the young "play" and bring an

extra life into the world with no sense of accountability. Often the parents who did not teach them to care for their childhood pets are now caring for grandchildren born out of wedlock. Sadly, parents do not hold their own children accountable for the new life and pick up the pieces just as they did with the pets years before. It appears that parents and grandparents make the same mistakes again and perpetuate the playing without paying the price. Parents could stop this cycle by making their own children accountable for their personal mess. If one participates in the process of conception, they ought to be obligated to support their progeny. No exceptions. No excuses! Yes, they may be young and need to finish school, but how will they ever learn if they do not accept responsibility for such serious behavior. There is no responsibility without accountability. Who will hold the young accountable and break the dysfunctional cycle?

Unseen Consequence of Moral Failure

At my elementary school one of the teachers had a scheme to exchange eggs for candy and sell the eggs to buy athletic equipment. This meant that all the children were bringing eggs to school from many sources. My cousin, Donald and I, decided to gather several eggs from my grandfather's barn and hen house and hide them by the gate. That night we dreamed of a big feast on candy bars.

The next morning on the way to school, we stopped by the gate to pick up our hidden loot and were discovered. Grandfather promptly marched us to the barn, cutting down a sassafras bush on the way. While he beat his pants leg with the bush, he called us chicken thieves. We protested that we had not stolen any chickens, just took some eggs.

Grandfather firmly declared, "There's a chicken in each egg. You steal an egg; you are a chicken thief." He never laid a hand on us, but the value of the lesson was heavy on our minds for years. Even today I often wonder, "If someone stole an apple, are they guilty of stealing an orchard?" Perhaps the children should learn a few more lessons from parents and grandparents about implicit crimes hidden in small acts of moral failure. Such lessons could benefit the dating game and the dysfunctional relationships that come from small ethical and moral failures. Maybe a good dose of common sense could benefit the young as they approach adult responsibilities.

The Lesson of the Stolen Pocketknife

When I was about ten years old, mother bought me a pair of boots that had a pocket knife in a little holder on the side of the right boot. Somehow I lost the little knife. After searching everywhere, it could not be found. Going to the Dime Store near my home and looking at pocket knives, with no money and an empty knife holder on my boot, I tried a knife in my boot for size. Something came over me. Why not just walk out of the store with the knife in my boot and no one would ever know? All the way home, my wounded conscience dealt with me.

The next day I returned to the store and replaced the knife, but didn't say anything to the store people. My conscience still was not satisfied. I returned to the manager and told him my story. He asked me to show him the knife. This I did and he said since I had been honest about it, he would let it slide. He also said he would put the knife up for me and keep it until I got the money. I gave him a nickel and returned each week until the bill was paid and the little knife was really mine.

Through the years I have often thanked God for my conscience and for the store keeper who understood the need of a little boy to have a knife, especially when his boot had a knife pocket. It is a good thing to trust young people when they take responsibility for their behavior. Raising children to respect others and their property is a required activity for a civil society. Adults should never miss an opportunity to teach the lesson of accountability.

Trial and Error System

Beside the children out of wedlock, the present trial and error system of dating and mating leads to divorce and more dysfunctional marriages that do harm to all involved as well as the community and society. The erotic-based, impractical serial mating process that involves multiple trial partners before the young settle on a marriage mate is obviously a disaster and could easily be described as an "accident waiting to happen." Research has supported a correlation between the number of pre-marital partners and post-marriage infidelity. Parents, extended family, faith-based groups, schools, community organizations, and governments at all levels must address this systemic and festering social dilemma if the nuclear family is to survive.

Bad Liaisons

Since two cannot walk together except they be in agreement, does society not have the ways and means to prevent some of the bad liaisons that lead to dysfunctional relationships, doomed marriages, and many abandoned and neglected children? Notwithstanding the proverb "an ounce of prevention is worth a pound of cure," this avoidable social tragedy is allowed to continue unabated and become a social and financial drain on family and community resources. Parents who out of love and mercy take in the innocent victims of their children's folly without holding the unwed couple accountable are perpetuating the problem and continuing the cycle.

When family resources are not sufficient or parents are unable or unwilling to clean up the children's mess, some are added to the welfare rolls, many need homeless shelters, and others walk the forgotten by-ways that lead to paradise lost, a human heartbreak hotel or a cardboard box on the street. This may well be the negative moral legacy of the twentieth century that could initiate a progressive social debauchery in the twenty-first century that would produce a valueless society and a lowest common denominator morality for human relations. The tragedy is that this moral decay and depreciation of the moral framework of the family was preventable.

Accustomed to the Moral Darkness

Perhaps the two World Wars, the Korean Conflict, and Vietnam did something to the moral consciousness of the world that dulled the awareness of ethical and moral failures. Maybe the recent civil wars, genocides and ethnic cleansing created a tolerance for inhumane and cruel treatment of others. Conceivably the eyes of the world have become accustomed to the moral darkness and unethical and immoral behavior has become acceptable as the norm. The 24/7/365 news cycle reports of corporate corruption and liaisons of presidents, senators, congressmen, governors, clergy, sports champions and other trusted officials has hardened the soul. In a country where some corporate executives steal from stock holders, where firemen start fires, where policemen commit crimes, where trusted leaders of faith-based organizations confess to moral failures, where clergy molest children, where it has become fashionable and acceptable to cheat on taxes, partners, and spouses, what can one expect of the next generation? What will be the ultimate outcome if someone does not stop the cycle of dysfunction? It must start by everyone teaching the young accountability and responsibility. There is no time to waste; delay could mean disaster for civilization as it is presently known.

Unintended Consequences

Notwithstanding the positive aspects of equal rights for women and minorities, there were unintended consequences produced by women's liberation, the sexual revolution, civil unions, and the cultural war against all that is moral and decent in society. In a nation filled with dysfunctional families and courts, jails and prisons crammed full of hard cases and people prosecuted for committing crimes against society, where is the outrage? Where the news is filled with crimes against children, spousal abuse, sexual abuse, battered wives, and abandoned, abused, and needy children, where are the policemen, the prosecutors, the judges who will enforce the laws on the books? In cities where the homeless are helpless, where the poor suffer with no relief in sight, where criminals go free and the victim continues to suffer both loss and humiliation, where are the authorities who could make constructive change? This is a kind of progressive debauchery that seems to get worse and worse. What can be done to turn the tide on a dysfunctional society? The best solution is to produce a loving relationship that culminates in a marriage with a home filled with love and children who are cared for and taught the right and proper lessons about life and the "birds and the bees." It could be done. It must be done!

A Three-Ring Circus

A two-ring ceremony should not become a three-ring circus filled with clowning, loud talk, and illusions. A good marriage relationship cannot be faked. Most everyone can see through the acting and insincere behavior. When a relationship appears to be one thing when in fact it is another, this false idea may deceive the mind for a moment, but it will never fool the senses. When true love is present it is evident to all. When artificiality exists in a relationship, it stands out like a three-dollar bill. There are three living things that one can never deceive about a love relationship. (1) One could never convince a stray dog that all dogs are loved when they are not; it doesn't matter how many times you say, "Nice, doggy!" The dog knows whether or not you like dogs. Just ask any postman. (2) A child can sense love and affection from the moment one enters the room; the lack of an affectionate relationship cannot be hidden from children. They know. (3) Old folk who have been around the block cannot be fooled by artificial smiles, unnatural touching, or small talk with someone you actually despise. The old folk sometime sense the dysfunctional feelings and behavior before the couple knows for sure themselves. The wise old folk cannot be deceived.

The Long-term Outcomes

We teach young boys to have certain deference for their mother, sisters, aunts, and grandmothers, but fail to teach them how to treat the girl next door or their best friend's sister. They cannot conceive the consequences of their hormonal rage or see the long-term outcomes of the notches on their pistol. What if a brother brings home a wife another brother formerly mated? What if a sister married a brother's best friend who had slept with every available female in the community? How would a sister feel when she discovered that her best friend had slept with her husband before her marriage? Would she not feel violated to some degree? Would she not be naturally outraged? These are some of the long-term outcomes of the present undiscriminating sexual behavior among the young.

What if?

What if a child born out of wedlock grew up to be your spouse and you discovered that your father was his/her father? What if you married a girl from the next town and on a visit discovered that she had slept with the whole football team? Offenders and their parents keep lots of this stuff to themselves, but at times it comes out to the heartache of others. It is similar to a time-bomb waiting to destroy the peace and quiet of a summer afternoon. Such discovery happens. Many a marriage counselor could tell stories that would curl your hair, but they are bound by confidentiality rules. This is why the marriage ceremony has the question "If anyone knows any just cause why this couple should not be united in matrimony, speak now, or forever hold your peace." This was designed to prevent the marriage of distant kinfolk and to prevent the problem of disadvantaged children being born to relatives. This is why the incest law exists and has been a social scourge on families for centuries. Decent and moral behavior of the young and old could prevent this plague on society. Tragically many of the facts about such promiscuity are locked away in a trunk of memories and the key discarded.

A Locked Trunk of Memories

When dating partners are not totally honest, the seeds of failure are both planted and watered. This propagative part of the past will produce a forest of sorrows. Although there are things others do not need to know, major episodes that could affect marriage should be shared. Honesty is the best policy in any relationship and without total disclosure one cannot make a sound judgment about a long-term relationship. Perhaps a mate's prying about old "sweethearts" is a dating distraction, but some aspects of personal "history" must be shared if a long-term relationship is planned. Men more than women often want to press for details, but no partner is obligated to fill in the blanks on events that happened before the current relationship began unless they have direct bearing on marriage. It should be remembered this train runs in both directions. Once a dating partner knows negative facts and still proceeds with the marriage it would be totally unfair to use the information against a partner in the future. Remember, patterns of behavior are often repeated. Be forewarned!

The pot cannot call the kettle black, but no partner wants to attend a party and meet a mate's old flame and be blindsided by the news, "Oh, we lived together a year when I was in college; it was nothing." That episode had been placed in the locked trunk of memories. With prior knowledge the incident may have been viewed differently and even understood. Yet, when there is a resistant pattern to sharing significant relationships that would have a bearing on a marriage relationship, it goes to integrity. It is best to put everything on the table. If it becomes a deal breaker it is better now than later. The journey through dysfunction junction to the destination called divorce is a disastrous trip that could be avoided provided the whole truth were known in time to make an objective decision about marriage.

Figure 4.1 – The journey through dysfunction junction to the destination called divorce.

If all the pieces fit and you work together
You can find a better way
To attract a worthy mate who will walk with you
To the end of the journey.

Chapter Five

The Problem With Words

Observing from a Distance

Observing my future wife from a distance for seven weeks, she sang in the choir, worked with young people, and served with the ladies auxiliary. She was always alone, so I decided she must not have a husband. Finally, with a little courage I shook her hand and asked, "Do you have a husband?"

She answered simply "No."
I responded, "Would you like to have one?"
Again a simple reply, "Yes."
I asked, "May we talk about it?"

She gave me her telephone number; I waited two weeks then called her. With the blessing of two families, the rest is a history of almost forty years of faithful companionship and partnership.

One Word Spoke Volumes

Early in our relationship and a few months before we were

married, I wrote the lyrics to a little tune based on something she said:

She said, "When we get married,
I'll be good to you.
When we get married,
My love will always be true."
So one little word made me happy,
One little word made me grin;
One little word from a special person –
That one word was "when."

English uses one Word

The word "love" was not mentioned - it was the one little word "when" that spoke volumes to me. The Greeks had four words to express love and affection, but the English language uses only one word "love" to express a large range of feelings of affection for people and things. The use of a single word "love" in relation to emotional feelings, affection, or attraction greatly complicates the dating and courtship process for the young. Young people often express "love" for another person when in fact it is a strong erotic desire and not the pure and unadulterated feeling of affection and respect. It is certainly not the feeling of respect one has for a parent or sibling. On the other hand, the Greeks were discriminating in expressing feelings about family, people and objects and used four different words to identify their level and direction of affection and emotional attachment to people and things. This discerning use of words facilitated a clear understanding.

Sacred Writings Originally not in English

Whether it was the early Christian history produced in Latin or the history of other religions in different languages, it appears Providence avoided the ambiguity of English. Could this be a reason Providence produced Sacred Scripture originally in languages other than English? The Hebrew Testament was in a language that had several ways to express love and affection: to love, to want, to like, to be loved, affection, favorite, amiable thing, in tennis "nil (zero) points", and slang "darling." The Christian Testament was originally presented in the Greek language? Common Greek certainly presents perceptive and practical words to clarify and judiciously express the meaning of concepts and constructs that are crucial to the understanding of human affective behavior and love relationships.

Four Greek Words

Agape was used to express the highest form of love, a one way attitude or affection of the heart that expected nothing in return. It was pure and unadulterated affection. When expressing friendship or personal attachment as a matter of sentiment or feeling, the Greeks used a form of *phileo* which was a kind of two way or mutual comradeship to express solidarity. ***Phileo*** was an expression of the head or mind while *agape* was an expression of the will or heart. For family and blood relatives the word ***stergo*** was used. A precise word ***eros*** was used to express sexual or sensual feelings for others. For some reason the word *eros* was not included in the Greek New Testament. Perhaps God intended modern mankind to build relationships on the basis of *agape, phileo,* and *stergo*, before considering *eros* or moving in the area of erotic interest.

Structured Gobbledygook

It is difficult to understand why the English language uses one word "love" to express not only feelings about other human beings, but it is also used for things, objects, and possessions. This complicates the early communication of young people and breeds misunderstandings and heartache. When a young woman hears the words "I love you" and understands it as an expression of genuine affection, but in reality it is structured gobbledygook and jargon for sexual desire, the relationship can become complicated. If couples were able to precisely express their emotions with honest intentionality in a relationship, and clearly understood the meaning of the words, acquaintance could become friendship and friendship could grow into companionship and companionship could mature into the solidarity of a lifelong commitment in marriage. Then dating and mating relationships would have clear meaning and be more honest and long-lasting; many of the dysfunctional aspects of relationship failures could be avoided.

Outside the Law

It is universally accepted that sexual expression and sensual feelings for blood relatives is forbidden and outside the law. The Greeks used *stergo* to express affection for close family and blood relatives. This further separated sexual *(eros)* expression from family and made sensual acts acceptable only between individuals outside the blood line, the implication is that such sexual relationships should have the knowledge and approval of the family.

1. ***Agape*** - (love) - one way love for ALL
2. ***Phileo*** - (like) - two way love for SOME
3. ***Stergo*** - (liberty) - approved affection from blood relatives
4. ***Eros*** - (lust) - sexual or sensual love for ONE

Order is Important

The order *agape-phleo-stergo-eros* is important; it suggests that a sound relationship is build on love, friendship, and family approval, rather than on a simple erotic interest. The *agape-phleo-stergo-eros* order appears to be an authorized process that produces an approved sexual relationship. Many couples by-pass the *stergo* step that provides family approval and go directly to *eros* and base their relationship on erotic interests, then the sequence *agape-phileo-eros* produces an acrostic that spells A.P.E. Could this order be a kind of "monkey business" or something less than genuine? Although it simulates an honest relationship, in reality it is an imitation and most surely not a permanent partnership. Marriage is difficult enough, but without the approval and assistance of both families, the relationship is considerable more difficult to maintain. When a couple literally starts at the bottom of the A.P.E. acrostic with *eros* (lust) and moves to *phileo* (like), then skips *stergo*, the approval of blood relatives needed to control the family circle, they may marry without the pure *agape* (love) attitude needed to hold a marriage together.

The Absence of *Eros*

The Greek New Testament used three of the words and constructs in many places to inform relationships with God, family and others, but the absence of the use of *eros* relative to erotic expression speaks volumes that few want to acknowledge. Since the urge for sexual expression and the need to reproduce is a dominant drive, why the absence of a discussion of *eros*? Does it mean that one should have *agape* "love" for all people in the world, even enemies? And out of all the people one "loves," choose some to (*phileo*) "like" and build friendship and enjoy fellowship? Then from those friends in the "like" category, choose one (*stergo*) to present to the family for approval and secure "liberty" for marriage. Once the vows are taken there will be plenty of time for the expression of (*eros*) strong desire and to build a sensual relationship.

Sacred Writings Informed Relationships

Does it mean that the New Testament does not inform sexuality or sensually-based attraction? Must one go to Genesis to find male and female articulation where they are told to be fruitful and fill the earth? Does the New Testament expression "in Christ there is neither male nor female" mean that sexual misconduct is not a gender issue? Rather it appears that sacred writings inform relationships and describe sexual expression and erotic feelings in one context as sinful and sexual contact in another committed relationship as sanctified. Since it is clear that the "marriage bed is undefiled," the converse would be true that sexual activity for the unmarried and the uncommitted could easily defile a relationship. Sex does not make things better; it makes things different.

> **Whereas**, the process and sacrament of marriage predates the legal ceremony recognized by the state;
> **Whereas**, the legal recognition of marriage is relatively new in history;
> **Whereas,** marriage was instituted to protect the wife and produce inheritance laws for the children;
> **Consequently**, does it mean that some in what are called "common-law" relationships are undefiled because of their long-term commitment to exclusivity?
> **Therefore,** it appears that the answer to the question of morality in the mating game is a long-term relationship and a lifetime commitment that sanctifies a union and produces a wholesome atmosphere for sexual expression, procreation, and family values.

Violation of the Rights of Others

Sexual activity without a long-term commitment becomes a violation of the rights of future family members. An unmarried partner may some day be another's spouse and someone's parent. Do individuals have the right to arbitrarily and haphazardly violate or infringe upon that future? Although such acts of consenting sex involving the unmarried may be called "fornication," in reality it is a form of infidelity and betrayal of future relationships. Everyone wishes to marry a pure and unspoiled mate and every child deserves unadulterated parents. When there are no serious commitments, vows of exclusivity, or completed plans for marriage, deceitful acts of intimacy are in reality not just fornication, but a form of implicit adultery. How could this be? It is clear from the words of Jesus that even impure intention is a form of implied adultery: You have heard the old commandment that one may not have carnal relations with another man's wife: 28. but, I say to you, he who casts his eyes on a woman with an impure intention has in his heart already broken the marriage vow. (Matthew 5: 27, 28 DNT)

Scripture Demanded Respect for Womanhood

Jesus' words on adulterating the marriage vows are perhaps the most searching words ever uttered concerning immorality. He declared that even an evil eye offends the heart and makes it guilty of immorality. The Law permitted the breaking of the family relationship by divorce, but Jesus pointedly stated that nothing should soil or in any way pollute marriage, the foundation of the family and the home. He did not say that nothing "could" weaken the foundation of marriage. This was viewed later as an ideal situation and exceptions began to creep into the sacred literature. This, together with a progressive decline in social morals, has brought the family to the depth of despair and created an animalistic promiscuity.

Scripture deals with being connected to family, to friends, and even being connected to causes. Relative terms are used to infer relation such as master and slave, husband and wife, father and child, neighbor and enemy, and the list goes on and on. Even the evils of immorality are presented in relational terms. Adultery was seen from the perspective of violation of the marriage contract by infringing on another's rights. With other opposition, fornication and the sin of keeping company with the harlot were classified as evil because of the absence of commitment to a lifetime contract. Both good and bad in scripture are viewed from a relational perspective. For example, if one hated his brother, he was guilty of murder or if one said he loved God and hated his brother he became a liar. And all liars are destined for hell!

Youth Sneer at Traditional Morality

In these days following the sexual revolution and the custom of sweeping youthful moral violations under the living room rug, overt promiscuity abounds. The young may scoff at the idea of traditional morality; yet, their animalistic behavior has brought nothing but heartache and pain to family and society. To correct the mistakes of the young, a family is often torn between abortion, adoption, or raising an illegitimate child while the perpetrator is relieved of responsibility. This moral dishonesty does not correct the problem; it simply relieves the young of accountability and permits them to "do it again." In reality it is good common sense for parents and grandparents to teach responsibility to the young and guide them in caring for their own offspring. By ignoring the obvious and justifying what is blatantly wrong they exacerbate the problem.

Perhaps if there is a parental penalty for such conduct it is the caring for and funding of the abandoned children. Although it is noble to care for an innocent child, especially when they are part of one's own gene pool, it should be remembered that the same upbringing which was given to the parent of the unwanted child is likely to be passed on to the next generation. The cycle could continue.

My personal knowledge is of a widowed grandmother who raised her illegitimate granddaughter; then raised the next great, granddaughter, then the next great, great, granddaughter who now has three children out of wedlock. The old grandmother is gone and there is no one to care for the children but the courts and the taxpayers. The road to disaster may be paved with good intentions, but good intentions are not sufficient to stem the tide of promiscuity. The parenting flaws must also be corrected before the cycle of immorality and illegitimacy can be broken. Who will teach the next generation? Who said we didn't need divine assistance to cope with the double whammy of excess *libido* and out-of-wedlock children?

Chapter Six

The Double Whammy

Unintended Consequences

The Eden Curse in the Genesis story was not only retributive justice for disobedience, but guidelines for protection of the human family. There were lessons that both the man and the woman had to learn if they were to survive in the hostile world outside the Garden. The serpent was punished, the ground was permitted to grow thorns and thistles that would complicate the man's work in feeding the family, and the woman was given pain in conception, pregnancy, and childbirth. In addition she was given the primary burden of caring for the young and managing the attending problems. This was not all...there was more! There were unintended consequences to disobedience that spread far and wide. The tidal wave of immorality that resulted from the disobedience in the garden has inundated families everywhere.

A Double Whammy

Tucked away in the divine indictment of the woman was a note that her "desire was given to her husband." Surely this was a broader concern than sexual *libido*, but certainly included the sexual component since other issues related to conception, pregnancy, and childbirth. This means in addition to the created male sexual desire, part of the females sexual desire was transferred to the man. The Hebrew word for "desire" means in the original sense "a stretching out after, a longing, a yearning, a desire." The word is used only three times in the Old Testament; twice it refers to the strong attraction between the sexes. First, it referred to sin and judgment (Genesis 3:16); then personified sin described as being like a crouching animal ready to pounce on Cain (Genesis 4:7); and finally in the contest of love and joy (Song of Solomon 7:10). This extra "desire" given to man has become a "double whammy" and may explain the strong sex drive of young men. It should enable parents to better understand the erotic pressures on the young that necessitate the need for strong guidance in how young men must conduct themselves and how they are to treat women.

A Kind of Jinx

This strong sex drive for the young is a kind of jinx with damaging consequences. Although it is an unseen force, the effect of the "double whammy" may have a negative outcome which can be controlled in all but a few cases. Sexual misbehavior should never be excused and those with an abnormality should be given medical assistance. This book does deal only with the normal sex drive of the young. The unintended consequences of indiscriminate sexual behavior among young males produce significant negative results for the family. Such promiscuity should not be tolerated, but it appears that a majority of society either sanctions or condones such behavior with no regard for cause and effect.

Addiction is a Disease

Sexual addiction is a disease that can be treated. However, this compulsion is somewhat more than a natural urge; if not condemned it is implicitly encouraged by various entities of society that have lost all sense of morality and ethical behavior. It is perpetuated by the courts that justify as a sickness what in many cases is simply licentiousness, reckless decadence or simply a lack of respect for women. This is a partial indictment of parents, cultural-specific institutions, the courts, and some faith-based organizations. It is time to seriously consider the antecedent causes of such behavior.

An Obvious Disregard for Morality

Based on court rulings in rape cases and in criminal sexual abuse of children, there appears to be a kind of official permission or approval for this behavior. Officials in government and leadership positions seem to regard sexual misconduct, even though it is considered immoral or wrong, in a tolerant way and this is done without overt criticism of the behavior. This appears to be an obvious disregard for morality and explicit ignoring of the shortcoming or moral faults of the young. Boys will be boys because men are not the fathers needed to guide them properly. Perhaps it is "monkey see; monkey do." This reminds me of a poem I heard in church when the children were misbehaving. The pastor stated:

With all the purring in the pews,
We can't blame the kittens new.
For making noise and trouble, too.
For copying what the Old Cats do!

Women are Blamed

From primitive attitudes to the modern media, women have been blamed for paradise lost without an indepth analysis of the issue. The men controlling most religions and cultures of the world established purification procedures following childbirth. These regulations for females after childbirth in various religions and cultures seem to hearken back to the Garden's retributive justice, but some scholars assume the purification rituals had something to do with the raising of children. Instead of seeing every woman punished following childbirth, some see the contribution and stress of raising children as a good reason for a period of contemplation after the birth of a child. Although most see this as a negative process, some understand that a mother is charged with the obligation to raise a son or daughter that will perpetuate her race, culture, religion and nation. Researching sociology in South America I discovered a small primitive culture where when a child was born the father had to take to his bed for 21 days to contemplate raising a child. Perhaps it is both a mother and a father who should give some serious consideration about rearing their children. Since it takes two to conceive a child, perhaps it was intended that two should do the upbringing of children.

A Chaste Mother of Grandchildren

Under Jewish law a mother who birthed a son had a period of purification or contemplation of 40 days, but the time was doubled for the birth of a female. Why the difference and double time? Did a female child's birth require more purification for the mother or was the contemplation of raising a daughter who would become a mother in Israel, the actual motive for twice the time of secluded contemplation. Since the Jewish religion claims the child to be the same faith as the mother, it is conceivable that the Jewish mother saw the double value as the purity of her female child and wished to raise her as a chase mother of her grandchildren. Could this be part of the reason the Nation of Israel remained together through centuries of persecution and finally in 1948 returned to build the State of Israel as a homeland?

Females Control Morality

If it be true that the morality of a society or culture is in the hands of the females, then the tradition of taking special care in raising female children is a good idea. If they are taught to be morally clean and chaste prior to marriage, they cannot be sexually corrupted by the action of local males. In fact, ten men may violate a young girl against her will and still not corrupt her character. Such an episode is traumatic for the victim but does not have to be a life-changing event. The acts of bad people do not corrupt others without consent. Moral corruption comes from within not from without. Victims of rape or incest should never be considered damaged goods because the damage does not reach her character and should not be permitted to destroy her future. However, it is evident globally that one corrupt and loose female in a community may corrupt many men. It is affirmed that all parents should give extra care in bringing up their female children. The future of society depends on the moral standing of the female. They must be taught the value of their childbearing capacity and then pass on this worth and significance to their own children.

More Care

Could it be a true that morality is in the control of the female whether she be a young maiden or a mature mother raising her children? If so, more care must be given to the raising and education of female children. They must be taught that the special child bearing equipment furnished them by Providence to produce children of their own in the context of a loving two-parent family. Young boys and men must also be taught respect for females and parenting skills so they understand the consequence of their actions. Young men must learn that the ability to procreate carries with it grave responsibilities and that both the pleasure and procreation function is under their control. As they are taught to respect their mothers, sisters and cousins, they must be taught to respect the neighbor's daughter and their friend's sister. Someday each of those females will be someone's wife and some child's mother. Every man expects purity in his wife and each child deserves a chaste mother. Young men must be taught to always remember these facts. No exceptions. No excuses.

The Right to Consent

The law respects all female's right to give consent or a formal permission for sexual intercourse. This is not a grunt or a mumbled sound. The law clearly stipulates that girls under a certain age **may not** legally give consent to sexual activity. Religion and morality recognize a time when a female **should not** give consent to sex even with a "promise and pledge of love." The law declares a legal age of consent and also declares that males may not force themselves on females of any age and; **if she did not give a formal consent, it is the crime of rape**. Such violent destructive treatment of females must never be condoned by a civil society. In the case of "date rape" it may be that the dating/mating game has become so systemic in society that casual dating is a risk and long-term dating a danger when there are no moral controls in place. Dating should not be just a social event; it should be considered a serious occasion that requires preparation and some clear-headed judgment.

A Bleak and Inhospitable Place

Forcing someone into sexual intercourse without consent carries punishment only when the victim is able and willing to testify in open court and endure punitive scrutinizing. A courtroom is a bleak and inhospitable place for a rape victim. The cruel truth is that the court and most present will blame her for "asking for it" and excuse the perpetrator with "boys will be boys." No female regardless of her past history should have to endure the double standard of being a victim and then being accused of instigating the crime in the process. It appears that the court system is stacked against the victim. This always send the wrong message to young men everywhere and sadly sends a message to the female that the male establishment will not believe you when you accuse one of their own.

The Female Tease

Parents must understand that daughters may become a tease and create an unwholesome dating atmosphere. When girls are permitted to wear improper clothing without parental restraints, the daughter may think it is "fun" to tantalize her date sexually. When parents choose not to remember that an erect penis has no conscience, there is combined responsibility for the consequences. When a tease says "no," it may be understood as "yes." Without formal consent the young male has responsibility, but was he instructed how to handle a tease or did the men folk in his family encourage his chances to get "lucky?" Who is to blame?

A Man's World

With little respect for women and the public's excusing of male offenses based on *libido*, little can be done to make the entrenched man's world into an environment that values family and individual rights. When the rights of anyone are violated, the rights of everyone are in jeopardy. When a child can be neglected, abused, and abandoned and no adult prosecuted for the crime, society is in trouble. If a clergyman can molest children and maintain a position of trust with the congregation and the community, what conduct may be expected of those who tolerate such a travesty? If there is no equal justice under the law, what happened to victim's rights? If terrorists have more rights, privileges, and perks than the homeless, where is the sense of justice or social guilt? What then is the criteria for acceptability in leadership positions or what standards may be used to prepare the young to select a proper mate?

Explanations of why they didn't
Make it to the altar or
Arrived as damaged goods!

Like a woman alone,
I was robbed by a mugger.

Like a lost puppy,
I was caught by the dog catcher.

Like the walking dead,
I was taken by the body snatchers.

Like a surfer on the net,
I was caught in the world-wide-web.

www. trap.com/online.dating/find.a.mate/games/

Chapter Seven

The Criteria For Acceptability

Search for a Proper Mate

The search for a proper mate requires both energy and time and some written guidelines. There are no speed limits on the road to good relationships, just a few rules of the road. Persistence is required to achieve excellence. Both the quality and quantity of relationships should be frequently evaluated. The marriage relationship is a way of life, not a theological scheme with which one must be in total intellectual accord. However, marriage is a realistic human endeavor and must meet certain criteria both public and private. This means the dating process must be selective and worthy of your time and effort. A cheap date may be a cheap date. Both males and females should carefully choose the persons they are willing to date. Remember my mothers rule "Never date anyone you would not want to marry." Some will say that narrows the field considerably. This is a good thing. Choose from the best and leave the rest to those who are not seeking a mate for life.

Acceptability

Criteria for acceptability for a proper mate are certainly more than physical attributes; beauty is only skin deep. Many of a mate's attributes cannot be observed by the eye but must be assessed by the senses based on a list of criteria. Divide the list into three parts: (1) those things that may be observed, (2) those things one must assess, and (3) things that would be a deal breaker. However, if you have not determined your acceptable standards you are not ready to date. You would not know whether or not a future mate met your criteria. Notice the word "perfect" was not used. Instead the construct of "proper" was stated. To be perfect is without fault, unspoiled, and just right in all respects. You will not find such a person; they do not exist.

Look at the best, choose two and pick the better one. The one who meets most of your criteria and the one in which you do not see a deal breaker. It is an intelligent process. Dating is not for the faint of heart. Dating is a stressful endeavor, but is also episodic; that is, a series of events complete in themselves form a part of a larger endeavor. This means that a dating partner may make a closure decision following each event or continue and make a decision after a series of episodes. If the decision is positive, that this is a person with whom you could live the rest of your life, then make marriage plans. If the decision is negative, bring closure to the relationship and stop seeing the person immediately.

Do not just marry a friend; marriage requires more that friendship. Why is friendship not enough? Friends are part of a group of people. Marriage is an exclusive relationship with one person. Friends need a group of people around them at all times or they become bored. Friendship can be used up much as money in the bank. When the principle and interest are gone the friends are gone. Marriage needs a partner with endurance and staying power. This is why the marriage vows include "for better or worse, richer or poorer, sickness or health." A spouse should become more than a best friend, more than a lover, more than a companion; hopefully, they will become a soul-mate that has a lifelong commitment to your welfare. True love is behaving in the best interest of a spouse.

Endurance and Forgiveness

No gain without pain and no long-term relationship without short-term difficulties that require endurance and forgiveness. All human beings have emotional weaknesses, physical frailties, and disadvantages. The idea of a proper partner for life is much less demanding than the perfect ideal in the mind of some. An appropriate mate is suitable, good, modest, courteous, but still a human being. If no deal breakers were found, genuine love would be able to overlook small things and develop genuine affection for someone in spite of human flaws. However, the more you know about the weakness of a future mate, the more objective you can be in choosing whether or not you can live with those particular faults the rest of your life. Yes, true love can love someone with a few faults, but not many. Personal shortcomings may be overlooked, but character weaknesses and defects that relate to integrity should become a deal breaker. Leave those with major flaws in the dating pool for those who are not seeking a life-mate.

A Baker's Dozen

Here is a baker's dozen of general questions that need to be answered about a future life-mate. Each person must add to the list their personal criteria.

1. What is their sense of family?
2. Do they love children?
3. What are their feelings toward their parents and siblings?
4. What is their politics?
5. What are their educational and professional goals?
6. What about religion?
7. How do they feel about shared responsibilities?
8. Do they habitually eat or drink too much?

9. What is their general health?
10. Are they ready to leave parents and cleave to you?
11. Do they gossip?
12. What about personal hygiene?
13. Do they have involuntary tics or quirks of behavior that annoy you?

Reasons vs. Purpose

Purpose is always singular. There may be several reasons for a relationship but a singleness of heart and hope should guide the construction of a purpose. Write it down and be clear what you want in a relationship. Be honest, if it is just sex almost anyone will do; you may throw caution to the wind--and reap the whirlwind. However, if it is a lifetime partner you want, then caution is the better part of valor. Purpose determines action and the general direction of a relationship. To construct an adequate purpose for a relationship, one needs to answer three interrogatives: what, why, and who. Once you know “what” you want, a mate for fun and games, a casual dating relationship or a serious marriage partner, and “why” you want the relationship, for sexual expression or long-term relationship and family, the final interrogative is “who” or “with whom” or more specifically with what kind of person do you desire this connection? Once these three basic questions are answered, one is ready to move forward with discretion, prudence, caution, and good judgment. A certain maturity is needed to be honest with yourself and others. Write all this down and then begin to develop objectives for the search. (Then talk with someone who knows more than you.) This would probably be your parents.

A Carefully Devised Plan

Objectives are a subset of the purpose and outline a strategy to accomplish the final intent. This carefully devised plan of action will guide the search for a proper mate. When each objective is reached there is movement toward the purpose. Objectives should always be plural because if there is only one it is simply restating the purpose. If you cannot subdivide your purpose into several objectives, your plan is not ready and you will make major mistakes. Premature entry into the dating/mating game can wreak havoc with both health and self-confidence. Discretion are the watch words for mate-selection.

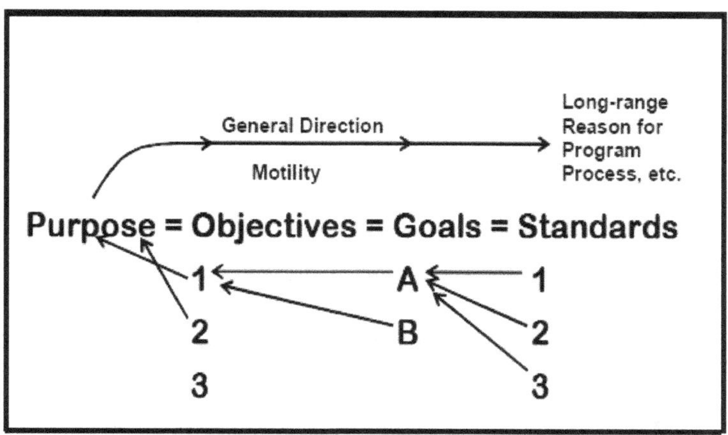

Figure 7.1 – A carefully devised plan of action.

Advancing the Purpose

When objectives are enumerated, the next step is to determine goals. They are plural also and two or more goals must be written for each objective. When these particular goals are met, then that objective is accomplished and the purpose is advanced. Next, one must determine acceptable standards or criteria to be used in making a decision or judgment about a long-term partnership. For example, in composition, an objective is clarity and the rules of grammar are used to determine the clearness of thought and expression. What are the criteria that will determine a proper mate? At what level of quality or excellence will you determine acceptability?

Be Honest

Once you make an initial observation and find out a “few facts,” make a decision whether or not this person remains on your list. If they do, then be up front and tell your date that you wish to have another chance to discuss the future. If the person is not interested in you and your future, then you will know. If they are, then you can begin to evaluate and assess the general qualities of the person based on the list you have made. If you seek a life-mate and the person has no "deal breaker" flaws, then begin a discussion as early as possible about a long-term relationship.

A Glimpse into the Future

There is a moment in any relationship that opens the door and provides a glimpse into the future. Does the person have a backbone? Are they able to stand by convictions? Do they have a sense of humor? One may be born with a backbone, but the funny bone and the wishbone are developed as one matures. Another issue is balance. Does this person bring balance and stability to your life? Do they have strengths where you are weak? Can your strength compensate for their areas of weakness? The objective is to find a mate who is compatible and similar in temperament. If you seem to be well-matched, then proceed with your plan. If you have the slightest question about any quality, make an objective decision. There are other fish in the sea. Would you be able to live with that particular weakness the rest of your life? Could one of your strengths compensate for that particular weakness or will it always be a bone of contention. Perhaps you should catch the next bus.

What about Widows and Widowers?

It is not those we love who make life worth living, it is loving that adds value to life. The absence of a loved one for any reason does not change the fact that they are loved; therefore, it should not change life except for the loneliness. Loved ones remain loved even after death. This may at times complicate the choice of a second mate after the death of a spouse. Or it may cause one to hesitate to marry a widow or widower. Yet, loving someone who has passed shows character and should not prevent loving someone who is alive. As long as there is love, life is worth living. The major problem with marrying a widow or widower is that the dead do not make mistakes. They are perfect. In such case make it clear that you do not wish to be compared to the dead but respect the fact that the chosen mate has a love strong enough to reach beyond the grave. That is a good sign.

What about a Divorcee?

This is another story. Ending a bad marriage is never easy. The old adage "breaking up is hard to do" expresses something considered to be a general truth. Memories are deep within the subconscious and remain buried for long periods just to surface when someone pushes a button that was secretly stored in the root cellar of the soul. Officially ending a marriage by a decision of a court is a public venue for a private problem, but there was no easy out. There are no winners; all are losers. The literature suggests that it takes from six months to about two years to get over a marriage breakup. If one chooses a divorcee as a marriage mate there is one simple rule: divorce is to separate or distinguish one from another; therefore, make it clear that a clean and complete separation must be made from the old life. The one exception is when children are involved. This must also be taken into consideration when marrying a divorcee.

Don't Be a Crutch

If you date someone who has lost a mate by death, divorce, or breakup, take care that you do not become a crutch. Why the crutch issue? It is obvious that when the healing from a separation is complete the crutch will not be needed. And the one thing desired in a relationship is to be needed by the other party for the right reasons. A few women are able to handle a breakup with strength and poise, but most men need a crutch to get through the anxiety and stress of the experience. When both my knees were replaced with titanium, knowing the recuperation period would include a crutch and eventually a cane, the doctor was asked "How long will I have to use a cane?" His simple response was "Until you forget it." No one wants to be forgotten. This is why one must not marry on the rebound. Let time do the required healing, then a new relationship can be established without the use of a crutch. Nursing a friend back to health is a worthy effort, but not the best way to find a life-mate. Sympathy and love are closely related and it is hard to tell the two apart. One must not marry to get another person out of a predicament; there must be genuine two-way love and enduring affection. To be discarded as a crutch is to be humiliated before family and friends. Your first responsibility is to take care of yourself.

The Bright Side

Although many marriages fail, especially the second ones, some individuals learn lessons from the loss and make necessary changes in attitude and lifestyle to get ready for a new relationship. Forgiveness and forgetting past harmful episodes brings strength to the present relationship. Everyone deserves a second chance. Look on the bright side. When two troubled souls meet, fall in love, and marry there is a new opportunity to get it right. This should spark an extra effort and could make things even easier. Provided no one pushes those secret buttons or makes the same mistakes twice. Human beings are resourceful and bounce back quickly from most human tragedies. That is the bright side. Learn the act of giving and receiving. Love takes time. Why not write a new and better chapter with a little forgiving and forgetting. Remember a burden shared is half as heavy and a blessing shared is twice as nice. Walk on the sunny side of the street and you can see clearly the need for a written document that could serve as a contract or agreement.

Chapter Eight

The Contractual Relationship

Prenuptial Agreements

Based on prior knowledge a couple should negotiate a reasonable contract that will endure. Discuss the whole matter with a future mate and consult a few trusted friends. Sure marriage is a personal matter but it has ramifications for family and friends. In the desire to wed often the unintended consequences are overlooked that may complicate matters and cause the desired result more difficult to achieve. This is why a contract is negotiated to work out in advance answers to anticipated questions or action in unexpected events. Prenuptial agreements are not only for the rich and insecure. Family assets should be protected and, if an inheritance or children are involved, concern for their future is required.

Human Contracts may be Broken

Relationship contracts are made between humans and can be broken. Marriage is contractual in nature and is based on a give and take balance. A contract is a drawing together through bargain or formal agreement to make a mutual commitment. Literally, a contract is a construct that abbreviates and narrows the issues, condenses the confusion, reduces the risks, and assures that certain agreed upon conditions will exist during the specified time of the contract. A contract to be binding must have a beginning and ending date. Normally, a marriage contract is "as long as you both shall **live**." Recently, some have requested a change in the wording that reads, "As long as you both shall **love**." Once the love and respect that brought two souls together is gone, the marriage is psychologically over and the distress and despair that predates divorce begins.

An Automatic Default

As an agreement or covenant between two or more parties, each person commits to do or not do something and acquires a right to what the other promises. In fact, it is a mutual promise or pledge made between individuals. It takes two to make a contract, but one can break it by not fulfilling the agreement. Action or failure to act may break the contract. When one party does not live up to the promises made, the contract is in default. Default is usually a failure to do something rather that action by one of the parties. One may fail to keep promise in a passive mode and also become unfaithful in an active mode. Sure reconciliation is possible and forgiveness is necessary for good mental health, but how many times must a spouse suffer a breach of contract? Reconciliation requires movement of both parties; in fact, it becomes a renegotiated agreement and perhaps should be put in writing. A failure to keep the agreements and vows is sufficient to produce an automatic default. The other party is injured and released from the contract. Those who keep their part of the bargain cannot alone keep the contract alive. All parties must fulfill their contractual agreements for the contract to remain valid and operational. Marriage partners must not compete; they are to complete each other.

Constant Bickering and Easy Divorce

A time existed in the distant past when individuals were encouraged to keep trying to make their relationship work, but now the opposite is evident. Constant bickering and easy divorce have brought havoc with the family life. Many marriages fail legally and others default emotionally with great damage to family and friends. The tragic evidence is that those associated with faith-based organizations have about the same failure rate as couples who do not practice a religion. This simply means that religion, even fervent personal participation in regular worship, does not guarantee one a stable marriage relationship. Evidently there are common factors in the human condition that impact all human relationship. Making a pledge, promise or legal contract does not provide the glue to hold a relationship together. Both parties must do regular maintenance and repair work for the relationship to endure.

Constant Effort to Maintain a Relationship

There must be constant effort by both parties to maintain a viable marriage relationship and that includes "time." Perhaps the fact of "time" has not been adequately considered. A secular couple depends too much on subtle and clever actions or words to influence their mate to remain in the relationship while those who practice a religion depend on some higher power to work the magic that will hold their relationship together without effort on their part. Neither scheme works. The old adage "love will keep us together" might work provided the couple used the same definition of "love" and were consistent in the practice and demonstration of affection. Even being hand-cuffed together in a locked room with no windows could not keep some folk together. One would probably just role over and die to escape an unfixable relationship. This may actually account for many of the medical issues suffered by some couples. So what and how must a "red-blooded" couple approach and maintain the marriage relationship?

A Good Place to Start

The beginning is always a good place to start. The first meeting is the last time to make a first impression. Look at the book of beginnings. God created mankind in His own image, male and female, and blessed them with the injunction to be fruitful and multiply; fill the earth and subdue it (Genesis 1:26-28). The idea of "subdue" suggests that there was hard work associated with living in a garden in a pristine paradise. Perhaps that is the problem with the marriage relationship, there is no one to do the hard work of controlling the growth of the jungle in which a marriage exists. No wonder there are so many weeds, briars, and thistles. Does this explain the pain and suffering?

Record of Personal Failure

Throughout sacred writings there is record of personal failure and over time even the family that God put together deteriorated and became dysfunctional. At the close of the ancient scripture, God said that He would send a Prophet who would turn the hearts of the fathers to the children and the hearts of the children to their fathers. The implication was clear, this must happen or God would strike the earth with a curse. (Malachi 4:6: Luke 1:17) There is plenty of evidence that the father/child relationship problem is worse; perhaps this is the curse of the failed marriage relationship. When marriage is dysfunctional, the children are characterized by an inability to function emotionally or socially and family values suffer greatly.

Without the Institution of Marriage

The Hebrew text (Proverbs 18:22) teaches a general principle "He that finds a wife finds a good thing." St. Paul adds "Marriage is honorable in all." Had the world been left without the institution of marriage as a moral safeguard to corral the unbridled immoral inclinations, civilization probably would not have developed as we know it. Scholars, who want to add to the Hebrew text the word "good" as a modifier of wife, forget that most wives were good in the first place and deteriorated living with a flawed husband. The facts are clear there are good and bad spouses and sufficient faults and failures on both sides for blame of any dysfunction in the marriage relationship. A moral failure is normally the failure of more than one person. It is often action and reaction that takes what one spouse does as license to make the same or similar mistakes.

Foundation Stones

One should clearly understand the foundation stones of relationship. Those stones are **accountability, responsibility** and **trust**. To be a functioning party in a contract, one must grasp the responsibilities and obligations with reference to the contracted relationship. A responsibility is an obligation to account for actions. Responsibility is specifically a response to the obligation to fulfill an agreement. It requires one to reply to another. Parties to a contract are responsible and accountable for the trust implicit in the promises they make to each other. These are the foundation stones of a relationship.

Contact, Compromise, and Contract

Relationships are based on an agreed upon contract that require a compromise. Originally, com/promise was a mutual promise coming from the word "com"- together and "to promise." The parties agreed to adjust and settle a difference by mutual consent, with concession on both sides and to surrender one's own interest to gain a benefit. It is similar to an agreement or covenant between two persons in which each party binds himself to do or forbear from some act. This is a bargain, a compact, a contract, or a mutual promise which binds the parties to a performance.

Relationship requires compromise, contract, and contact. The initial contact is exciting and romantic because it is new and different. Because of individual differences, there must be compromise. This is not a bad word; it simply means "com" together with "promise" or together promise. Each party must give up something to get something and this is called a contract. This contact normally takes the form of soliciting favor. It is marked by civility and elegance of manners. When this contact has the motive of a love relationship, it is fragile and thrives on the edge of disaster. One slight change and it could fall apart and be forever lost. No human being is perfect and at times human failures sneak into a relationship. To maintain the adrenalin levels of courtship which exists with the threat of disaster is impossible.

Yet, most individuals in personal relationships have hopes that this stage will last indefinitely. To expect the excitement and adventure created by the fragility of early courtship to continue is unrealistic. Yet the effort to maintain the passionate sentimentality of a courtship is quixotic and deceptive at best. Constant contact, occasional consecration, straight-thinking, sensible actions, deferential behavior, and demonstrated affection are required to keep the passion in a relationship. And passion has its own excitement that produces the glue of attraction and delights the soul sufficiently to keep the home a happy place for family and friends.

Removing the "R" from Contract

A contract is a compromise so do a little compromising. Keep your promises because your word is your bond. This requires working on a relationship. It is easy to relate the social construction and the legal agreement of a marriage arrangement with a contract. When the "R" (Relationship) is removed what remains is the word "contact." Some socio-historic critics of marriage easily link the marriage contract with a negative implication of the word; such as, "contract a disease, become infected with a virus or come down with a fever." With the perspective of so many failed marriages and the host of dysfunctional relationships one can easily see a reason for the negative view. However, when trouble comes because the "R" was removed from the contract, one still has the word "contact." This suggests get in touch with, call, speak to, and establish communication. Could the negativity be overcome and the institution of marriage restored to its pristine place in society by proper "contact?"

Disagreements and Differences

Two individuals in close proximity will encounter conflict. There will be disagreements and differences. Arguments and quarrels grow out of discord and tension and contradictions fuel the fires of dysfunction. Married couples may be family, but they come from different gene pools, different upbringing, different experiences and are not blood relatives. The only blood connection is through their children where the same gene pools are combined. They have a contractual relationship. One can break a contract by overt action or passive failure to keep a promise. Broken relationships are more difficult so why even try to fix the problems? Because a contract is a covenant and it is more valuable than a relationship coming from birth. "Blood is thicker than water" relates directly to the "leave and cleave" principle in Genesis. This phrase suggests that a spouse is to support a mate even against mother and father, siblings or even their own children when there is conflict in the family. This phrase has completely lost its original, covenant-related meaning.

Today, "blood is thicker than water" is interpreted as meaning that blood-related family members are to be considered more important than anyone else. This behavior may cause a spouse to feel deserted by the person who was supposed to be their best supporter. However, the original meaning was, "The blood of a covenant (contract) is thicker than the water of the womb," meaning the contract with those with whom you are joined in a covenant relationship is to be considered of more value than blood relatives or the relationship with siblings with whom either may have shared the womb or relatives with whom either may share a gene pool. It appears from history that people take contracts seriously. Married folk should also see their agreements before God and man of sufficient significance that they work through differences and disagreements without interference from family members. However, marriage is not a prison or a black hole where nothing escapes. A spouse who fails to support a mate during a disagreement with family members will soon discover this fact.

Marriage is a Blessing

Notwithstanding all its dysfunction and embarrassments, the marriage relationship is a blessing. In most cases, a soul mate is better than being alone, because celibacy overtime is abnormal and requires a consecration that most are unwilling or unable to make, especially in the sensual society of sexual liberation. Research has demonstrated that married men live longer than single men, probably because of the love and care of a wife and the absence of dysfunctional behavior that comes from multiple sexual encounters. At creation it was clearly stated, "It is not good for man to be alone." St. Paul made it clear to the pristine church that it was better to marry that to attempt to contain passion. Marriage can be a blessing that brings morality and stability to the family.

Solomon may have overdone marriage and concubinary just a smidgen, but as a wise man he stated: "Two are better than one, because they have a good reward for their labor." He continued to write about the difficulty of keeping warm on a cold winter night sleeping alone. From the record it appears that he thought one was not enough. What does this prove? Even the wise and the wealthy make foolish mistakes. Solomon also wrote, "Better is a poor and a wise youth than an old and foolish king, who will no longer be admonished." To admonish is to advise someone to do or more often, not to do something. Couples must learn from their mistakes and admonish the young to break the cycle of dysfunction; however, if Solomon were correct don't waste your time attempting to admonish the old and foolish. There is no fool like an old fool! To be forewarned is to be forearmed.

Demand Drastic Changes

The dating/mating/marriage sequence demands drastic changes. An affirmative response would demand significant changes in the courtship and dating game and in the process of marriage relationship. Someone must build a better spouse trap, learn from past mistakes, change present attitudes, and teach the next generation a better way to find a proper mate. It is assumed that the shallow and sensual approach to dating is the culprit in a dysfunctional marriage. Of course, there are other factors, but it is assumed that the dating/mating process is the primary culprit. It is this sensual approach to relationships that causes a marriage partner to stray. There must be other reasons why relationships fail, but sexual activity seems to be the major cause of record. All must be addressed if the institution of marriage survives as a restraint against immorality and remains a safe place to bring up children and enjoy a growing family.

The dynamics of relationship are varied and can be easily misunderstood. The misunderstanding comes from both the force of basic motives and the actual activities that influence individuals into certain behaviors. Dynamics are the forces and powers operational in any relationship. Love is a choice. Marriage is a covenant. Relationship is a two-way street with lots of traffic. Love is a rough journey on a rugged trail with the summit out of sight. Love is a pursuit of happiness that searches diligently until it finds a person who brings a degree of satisfaction to life and living that permits pauses in the journey for a drink of the cool water of encouragement. Some see this as the pursuit of happiness.

The Anatomy of Relationship

The heart of the matter relates to how the parties understand the anatomy of relationship. The word “relationship” suggests several things: connection, association, harmony, affinity, and rehearsal. In fact, the word has a specific meaning that has little connection to the common usage. If one clearly understood the meaning of the word, it would be easier to accommodate the concept into daily life. When the word "relationship" is broken down, it means "re" again, backward, anew, over again; "la" look, "tion" conveyance or being to create or make and "ship" create, make or show status or quality. Put it all together and a working definition of relationship building would read:

Relationship is looking back, again and again, to renew those things conveyed to create agreed upon things and to determine the status. Is the partner a friend, a partner, an associate, an acquaintance or soul-mate? The looking back again and again is to assess the standing and to be certain that the original promises, spoken and unspoken, are being kept by both parties and making the necessary adjustments to the working agreement.

Relationship is not a Self-propelled Entity

Relationship is not the love boat but a sailing ship named "Hope for Tomorrow." Love relationships are similar to a "sailing ship" that is not self-propelled; sailing ships have either external force applied to properly set sails, or some power to produce forward motion in addition to the self-effort of a crew of two. Relationships are not easily manipulated by individuals but are similar to a ship of grace sailing on the sea of time and must have a cooperative crew and favorable winds or it is sure to run a ground or sink in the storm of neglect. Contrary winds and shallowness are the usually culprits that cause a shipwreck on the rocky shore of Sorrow Island in the Sea of Neglect.

The Scheduled Port of Call

Relationship is not a love boat powered by some modern engine and guided by the best radar available. After the dating is over and the ceremony has past, marriage becomes an unfinished sailing ship that must be equipped with sails and rigging. If the rigging is makeshift, done in haste, it will not hold in the coming storm. Not only so, the crew must know how to set the sail in a crosswind to move forward toward a safe harbor. It has been said that the hand that rocks the cradle rules the world. This may be true, but in a relationship as in a sailing ship the sails that must be properly set for contrary winds and the crew of two must work together to survive. A sailing ship was not built for smooth seas; it was designed to encounter the harsh even anticipated storms. This ship for two is not just a pleasure boat for sunny cruises and parties with friends, but a working boat built to carry family cargo and crew safely to a secure harbor without excess baggage. In fact during the first storm at sea most of the old baggage must be put overboard for the ship to make any safe port. Once the storm has passed the ship must be rigged again for contrary winds to make the scheduled port of call.

Good Advise from Old Sailors on the Dock

It does not require a professional to obtain good common sense advice about relationships. Enter any place where sea-going folk gather and ask questions about preventing a dysfunctional relationship journey and many answers would be forthcoming. Here are some selected gems worthy of a copyright from the old sailors on the dock:

© Always show affection when you meet.
© Never neglect your spouse sexually or socially.
© Learn from mistakes and leave them in the past.
© Settle all arguments so you can rest before the next storm.
© Learn to forgive and forget past failures.
© Admit and correct your personal mistakes.
© Enjoy the present moment, trouble will come.
© Earn respect and respect others.
© Always speak softly except during a storm, then say nothing.
© Listen and set your sails properly for contrary winds.

Everyone Needs Help

Scheduled to speak to a leadership group at the Rolls Royce

plant in Derby, UK the week the Super Sonic Transport, SST Project went bankrupt. Rolls Royce made the engines and Lockheed was constructing the air frame. Both went under and needed government bailouts. After the address my tour included the plant making the SST engines. They were so large several men could be seen working inside the engine. There were small fan blades on the front of the engine and the guide was asked if I could have one. "Whatever for, sir?" I said, "If big companies such as Rolls Royce and Lockheed need help, we all need help. My intention is to make a plaque and place a piece of this engine on it and call attention to the fact that "Everybody needs help."

He told me all parts were classified, protected by heavy security, and numbered and must be accounted for each shift. Broken pieces must be melted down and the material reused. It is a special material and spies have been arrested just the week before and deported for trying to get pieces of this engine. The next morning in my hotel box was a small plain brown envelope filled with cotton. Inside the cotton was a small fan blade. The plaque was made and it reminds me that we all need help now and then and should never be reluctant to ask for support from those able to provide assistance.

A Final Epitaph

Entering a nice restaurant and ordering a well-done steak, my patient waiting was interrupted by a rare steak. It was returned to the cook and then returned again still medium rare. My patience was wearing thin so a message was sent to the chef. "Tell the cook that I am a man of God and he will never get to heaven!" This bought the chef out of the kitchen to my table. "Sir, you don't know me. Why would you say such a thing?" My answer was clear, "Scripture says that everyone who makes it to heaven will hear 'Well, done thou good and faithful servant.' This steak was returned three times and you didn't get the message –well done!" With this the chef smiled and my well-done steak arrived with a special garnish. Everyone wants to hear that they have done well. What will be the final epitaph of your relationship journey?

Bringing spiritual assistance into relationship building may provide safe passage through the darkened woods of dating without too many skirmishes and scars. Failed relationships hurt because even brief disagreements leave bad memories that surface occasionally to disturb one in the dark. This may cause one to question themselves, "What could I have done differently? What could I have done better? What must I do better the next time?" Both an emotional and a spiritual grounding may bring partial answers to such questions; however, relationship building is an ongoing and developing process. By the time you get it right, it will be time to step through the pearly gates. Surely, everyone on that side of Jordan will be happy and enjoying family and friends. Otherwise, according to most religions those "bad folk who caused all the trouble on earth" are going to have a miserable time down there. That is unless my friend is correct when he said, "I know things will be better, because I have already had my "hell on earth." He described his marriage journey as a passenger on the slave ship "Broken Promises" that sailed rough seas for three decades. And as an after thought he said, "There was no one who could or would assist us through the troubled times."

No Third Party

It makes one wonder if he had looked beyond his mess and sought assistance from a power higher than himself. I know what that particular person would say, "Even God couldn't fix our problems so why bother him? We made the mess ourselves and both of us behaved in a way that made things worse. We probably would not have taken the advice of even one who rose from the dead. We did avoid bringing others into our problems, but we never really considered an encounter with God."

The EVERGREEN Devotional New Testament (DNT) deals with the general issue of kind words and proper response to others in order to assure **a well spoken eulogy at the end.** A eulogy usually comes after death, but it is written long before the end actually comes to life.

Called to Give Kind Words
1 Peter 3:8-12 (DNT)

8. Finally, you must think the same thoughts, suffer with one another, having automatic interdependence with brotherly kindness; be tender-hearted and humble-minded: 9. you must not repay injury with injury, or hard words with hard words, but bless those who curse you. For you were called to give kind words to others and come to a well-spoken eulogy at the end. 10. For the one wishing to love life and see prosperous days, let him avoid an evil tongue and cunning words. 11. Habitually avoid evil, and do good things; let him seek and follow peace. 12. Because the eyes of the Lord watch over the righteous, and his ears listen to their prayers: but the Lord looks directly into the eyes of wrongdoers.

Chapter Nine

The Triangle Encounter

Transition Dynamics

In the dating game there is always a third party standing in the wings. Do you know about the "little black book" filled with names of alternates should others fail to perform adequately? The construct of transition dynamics suggests that change is a powerful force moving everything in its path as it passes from one condition, stage or place to another. Dynamics are the change-producing forces that cause the activity that produces change in any situation but particularly the relationships between people. The tendency is toward change; nothing will stay the same so change will come if one acts or does nothing. All change is not good, but some change is actually progress. In human relations one must expect and be prepared for change. When it comes, change should not be taken personally. Embrace the change and flow with the force as long as it is constructive.

Change will provide a new perspective on life and living. Change can bring improvements. It is normal to want things to stay the same, but that is not reality. Change will make things different; they may not be better but at least one will not become bored. In fact the forward movement will give one more control in directing the change in the direction one wishes to go. It is similar to steering an automobile. If the car is moving, it is much easier to steer. So do not fear change; embrace and control what you can for the benefit of your relationship.

Since Euclid Wrote about Triangles

Triangles have been used to demonstrate various aspects of two-dimensional life since Euclid wrote books around 300 BC. The interior angles always add up to 180 degrees or one-half of a circle; therefore, if two angles are known one can easily determine the third angle. The sum of the exterior angles, one for each vertex is 360 degrees of a full circle.

A Drastic Difference

The marriage relationship differs drastically from the dating sequence. Marriage is a two-dimensional figure formed by three sides and three angles. The triangle is a fundamental figure of geometry since it is a polygon with the fewest sides. A two-ring ceremony of marriage vows, made to God and a partner, should become an equilateral triangle with three sides and three angles. The old saying that three is a crowd is not true in the case of marriage. When a couple chooses to bring Providence into their working relationship they have an ethical and moral grounding. In Western Civilization a couple is married in the eyes of God and should function with that perspective. If Providence is a part of the marriage the couple has a better chance to achieve a healthy and productive relationship. It is a chance, not a guarantee, perhaps even a probability, but without certainty. Much depends on the labor of the participants. This reminds me of a story from my grandfather.

My grandfather Green was a religious man who trusted God. He was primarily a farmer but also an amateur herbalist and horticulturist. One year he showed his distinguished crop of corn to a city slicker. The fellow thought grandfather was too proud of his own labor and told him to be grateful to God for providing the soil, the sunshine, the rain, and in reality it was God who made the corn grow. After listening to the exhortation grandfather retaliated;" I know God is working, but you should have seen that field when God had it by Himself! He sure left a lot for me to do." And so it is with relationship building.

Marriage is a Garden

A marriage relationship is similar to a growing garden. What does it take to grow a garden? First, there is diligent preparation and cultivation of the soil where the garden is to grow. Next, comes careful and prayerful planting of the proper seeds. Then, comes the requirement of unceasing effort and constant attention during the growing season. Finally, the garden must be blessed with sunshine and rain and touched by the invisible hand of Providence. Some external circumstances may be outside the control of the garden keepers; however, the invitation for direct intervention by Providence is clearly within the purview of those managing the garden. Good judgment and foresight in the management of a growing marriage relationship should also include the acceptance of divine guidance.

Legitimizes the Family

It should be remembered that a married couple are joined in a two-dimensional, civil contractual arrangement. This contract is (1) first, it is a formal agreement to unite with another person for life under rules and conditions established by the ethics and morals of society; (2) second, it is a contract signed by both parties and registered with the state as a legal document and becomes an agreement to live together in a single domicile and become productive members of society. It is this legal arrangement that legitimizes the relationship for society, the family, and creates an atmosphere conductive to the nurturing of children. In addition to the legal aspects of marriage, it is desirable for couples to be brought together in an ethical and moral manner that is in keeping with the long-standing, faith-based principles for marriage.

Draw a Triangle

Draw a triangle and write "God or goal" at the apex (A). On one of the base angles write your name (B). On the other base angle, write the name of your spouse (C), or if you are presently single, write the name of a significant other with whom you desire a long-term relationship. Then place your two index fingers on the base angles, and move them up the sides toward the top. Notice how the two move closer to each other as each one moves closer to the apex. As a couple moves closer to God or to their established goals they become closer to each other. The converse is also true. With a solid base relationship, you can then reach forward (D) to others. This also works on the materialistic side when the term goal is used and the same vertical and horizontal procedure is followed. As two individuals move closer to the apex, they become closer together. Sacred writings asked, "Can two walk together, except they are agreed?"

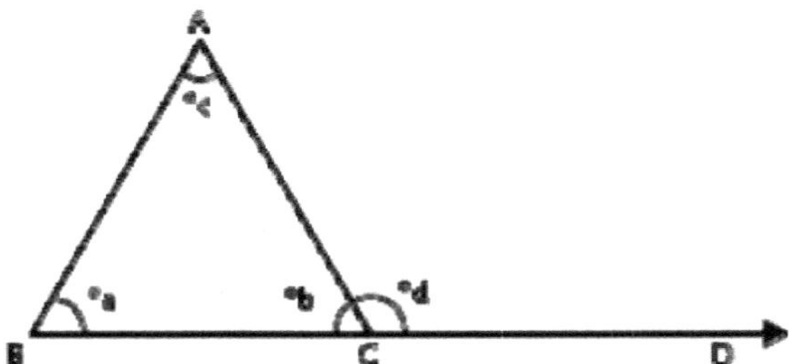

Figure 9.1—A vertical and horizontal relationship.

However, if a couple drifts away from either the moral and ethical principles included in the marriage contract, or they fail to progress toward their life-goals, the two will drift apart and the dysfunction begins. Should this occur, the couple may need to reaffirm their marriage vows or renegotiate the marriage contract. (See Chapter Twelve)

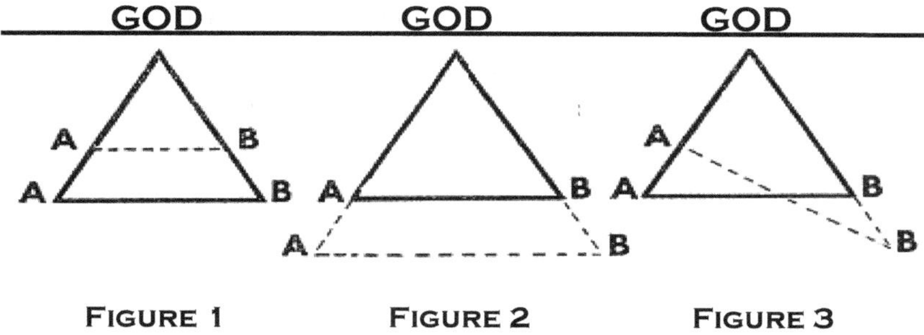

TRIANGLE RELATIONSHIP. The relationship between A and B illustrated here is in direct relation to their relationship with God. Figure 1 shows that as A and B get closer to God they are closer to one another. Figure 2 illustrates the strain in human relations when both A and B drift away from God. Figure 3 shows the change that takes place when A draws closer to God and B drifts away. This situation often complicates both the spiritual life and the human relations of A and B.

Figure 9.2 - The Triangle Relationship
Source: Green, H.L., Discipleship, ISBN 978-0-9798019-5-8

A Right-Angle Relationship

A good relationship may well depend on the right angle made when the two straight lines of individual behavior meet and form a right angle toward the apex. The right triangle has one angle that is a right angle; that is, the vertical line is perpendicular to the base line and forms a right angle. Rather than trying to be equal it might be better to be right especially in relationship to God and goals set by one's spouse.

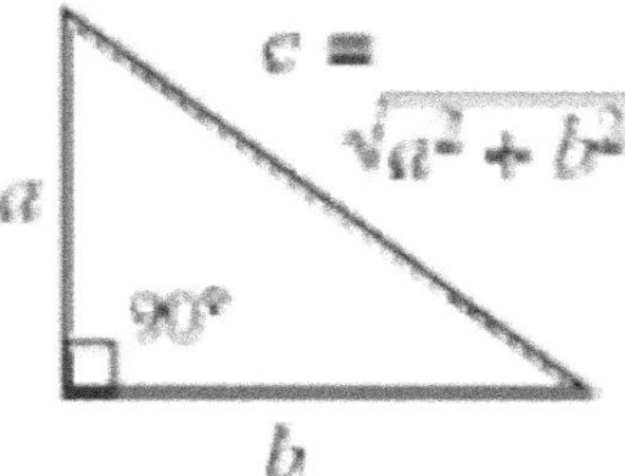

Figure 9.3 – Right-Angle Relationship

Note the line from the apex to line (b) would be the direct influence of Providence or the power of goal setting dynamics.

If one used the right triangle to illustrate the relationship with another person with a power other than self and also having an extended relationship with others, the best sacred writing (1 John 1:7) clearly pictures two walking in light and power from the apex and as a result developing fellowship with one another and with the force itself. In fact when one has a right-angle relationship with Providence or share mutually established goals, others are seen in a different light and this makes partnership and camaraderie much easier. This produces solidarity in a relationship unequaled in human companionship and camaraderie suggests an intimate, loyal, and good-spirited partnership. A relationship must be built on mutual respect and a grand pursuit of happiness. The excitement is in the pursuit, the chase, the ultimate objective is never reached, but the effort continues and that is the joy of living together in a sound relationship. The founders who composed the American Constitution wrote about the "pursuit of happiness" that was a guaranteed right of all. Claim your part of this provision and walk with your mate in pursuit of the goals that will bring mutual happiness.

Find the Center

The center controls the whole circle of relationship and is the main part of and the middle point that forms the circle around a marriage. To find the center one uses three points. Measuring from the apex and the two angles that complete the triangle one may find a center point. It will most likely be self, sex, or a spiritual emphasis. One will be the primary point or the controlling force in the relationship the other two will factor into finding that center or point of reference. Otherwise there will be a wobbly satellite destined to fall and be consumed by the hostile atmosphere.

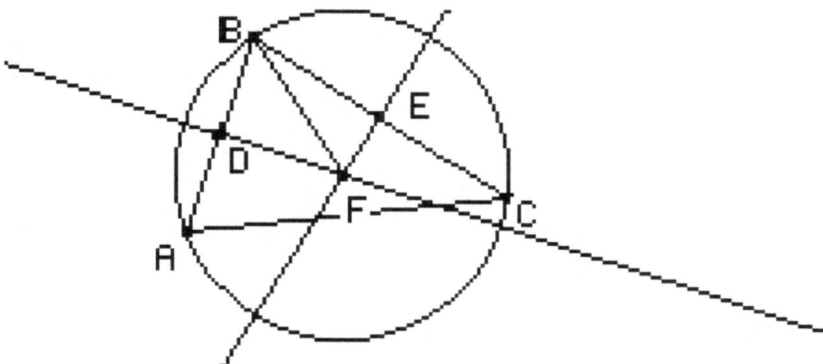

Figure 9.4– Enclose a circle about a central point of a relationship.

A Wobbly Satellite

The marriage relationship could appear much as a wobbly satellite destined to fall into the consuming atmosphere, except when the central control is strong enough to hold the relationship together by enclosing parameters around the controlling point. This would provide stability. However, should self become the controlling factor the relationship will become unstable, unpredictable, and even erratic. If sex becomes the primary control, the relationship will be short-lived. However, provided the locus of control is a spiritual emphasis or agreed upon faith-based principles and goals, and others are left out of the circle, the relationship should become stable and maintain a permanent orbit above the cares of life that so easily overwhelm a weak marriage relationship.

Technical Procedure

Construct the perpendicular bisectors of two sides of the triangle. This can be accomplished by following the basic perpendicular bisector construction. Select segment AB. Place a midpoint on AB. Label it D. Select the midpoint D and segment AB; use the perpendicular line and construct a perpendicular at D. Select segment BC and repeat the steps, but label the midpoint E. Label the point of intersection of the two perpendicular bisectors point F. Construct segment

FB. Once the center is found, the circle may be constructed. Using the center + radius construct a circle with center F and radius congruent to segment FB. Knowing and understanding the role of the center is essential to an adequate relationship. Whichever point is the center (self, sex, spiritual) will control the other factors and keep them either in balance or out of balance. An out of balance relationship will deteriorate and ultimately fail.

Application to a Relationship

The technical procedure has a practical connection to relationship building. With (B) being the apex power/influence and (A) being spouse A and (C) being spouse (C) find the midpoint on line AB and CB which is relational connection to the apex and label the midpoints of AB (Destiny that relates to Providence) and CB (Eternity that relates to perpetuity). Then construct a line perpendicular to line AB at point Destiny and a line perpendicular to line CB at point Eternity. Label this point of intersection of the two perpendicular bisectors point (F) (Future). This is the midpoint of the circle that is constructed from the midpoint of the couple's relationship to the apex which will determine the Future of the relationship. Now the center has been determined. Next construct line (FB) to connect the Future to the apex and this becomes the radius that determines the range of effectiveness or influence that holds the relationship together. Notice that this establishes a relationship between (Destiny) providence and (Eternity) perpetuity. Relationship is a limited circle that contains only the couple and the influential power source and excludes all others who are not signers of the contract or partakers of the covenant agreement. This is where the leaving and cleaving enters a marriage relationship. Now this relationship is on solid footing with providence and perpetuity connected and unless some outside force intervenes to disturb the "perfect union" things will go as well as humanly possible until death suspends the earthly part of the journey.

Elements Competing for Control

Find the center of the circle of relationship. There are three competing elements striving for control of the relationship triangle. These are (1) Self as a **controlling factor** deals with personality, character, and individual identity as **central** to the relationship, (2) Sexual expression used as a **coping mechanism** must be secondary to the primary control and must not become a gender issue but always relates to both partners and whether or not the maintenance of the relationship would **collapse** without sex, and (3) Spirituality as the **crucial deciding factor** in a faith-based expression as the **core** of the devotion and affection between the couple. Just as the Creation Trinity are three in one; so self, sex, and spirituality combine to create one relationship that is either good or bad. It depends on the relationship controller that encircles the couple. This means the couple must agree on which of these three forces will be in the driver's seat and which ones will be the backseat drivers offering suggestions from time to time. This depends on which one of the three is strong enough to control the relationship and be used to enclose and limit the size of the relationship circle. Remember there will be enough conflict among these three without adding others to the mix. Keep the issues inside the circle.

Circle of Human Experience

The full circle of human experience and marriage relationship is divided into two half-circles. The starting point of the **first half-circle** of human experience is the individual. One either thinks of self or of others and this is determined by one's character. In the first half-circle of human relationships one usually uses others for selfish advantage. There is little or no regard for the privileges and rights of others when it distracts from personal desires. The "we" of joint activity may only be the enlargement of the "I" and not really mean anything. A group task may be credited to the leader with no mention of those who actually did the work. In this half-circle, everything seems to focus on the personal desires of the individual.

In the **second half-circle** of human experience one relates to others. The essence of an individual is not found within the self, but in sharing life with others. Fulfillment is found only in meaningful association with others. Proper relationship with other persons is basic to the whole circle of human experience and activity. The essential nature of man is one with one and life has meaning only through continued involvement with others in mutually related tasks. A healthy individual in right relationship with the divine and self cannot maintain a normal existence in complete solitude. The essence of one's spiritual experience cannot long remain a solitary thing. There must be a sharing with others. The need is to construct a mutually satisfying relationship with another human being. The most acceptable way to do this is the marriage relationship that produces a family.

No Mountain High Enough

There is no mountain top or pinnacle high enough to see the whole of the marriage relationship. Most of the many voices raised on the marriage question contain truth. Each may see a different part of the whole picture, but no one is able to rise high enough above their own cultural limitations to see the whole picture. Each approaches the sacred relationship in their own way out of their own cultural perspective. Certainly honest men hold irreconcilably different beliefs about the marriage relationship, but they all claim to be moral or faith-based views. Perhaps there is a need for a practical view of the marriage relationship.

The Adulterated Vows

Marriage is a social and lawful relationship and when this union is between believers it becomes a spiritual partnership. Regardless of the religious issues, when two adults join themselves together in matrimony; this is an adult behavior. A true fact is that adults are human and are not perfect; consequently, corrupt behavior can violate the marriage vow and place in jeopardy what appears to be a near perfect union. When either attitude, a predisposition to act, or behavior, a goal directed activity, interfere with the harmony between a married couple, the relationship may become adulterated. To adulterate is to debase or make impure by adding another ingredient or substance of poor quality to the mix. When that ingredient is an infatuation with another sexual partner it is called adultery. In reality, it is simply adding another person to the joint venture called wedlock. Almost any manner of lewdness or unchastely behavior can form a key that unlocks the binding force called wedlock. Three is a crowd and a paramour can easily break-up a partnership. Yes, it is true that a person my actually love their spouse and still become unfaithful. It happens to moral and ethical people just as often as it does to those of low character that everyone abhors. Why does this happen?

Defilement and Adulteration

Defilement of the marriage bed happens when touching stops, communication breaks down, courtship cools off, cash is in short supply, or when the cares of life are multiplied beyond normal range. Some well meaning folk seem to believe that "wedlock" means the marriage ceremony locks people into a permanent relationship. This false assumption also breeds an infallible syndrome that the marriage cannot fail because it was made in heaven and blessed by the church. In reality "wedlock" is an old Anglo-Saxon word combination from "wed" meaning a **pledge** and "lock" meaning **a gift, a token.** The ceremony normally includes "In pledge of the vows between us, I give you this ring." When a bride and groom "pledge their troth" they are making a solemn vow to remain faithful for the duration of life. When a marriage partner seeks comfort or excitement from someone other than a spouse, then they have added another and the marriage vows are adulterated.

Libido vs. Albedo

Libido is the sexual urge or instinct that has become the driving force in human relationships. As an aspect of a lustful nature, it becomes negative in execution; consequently, it offers no building blocks for a relationship. Sex does not make things better; it makes things different. When sexual expression is a biological function rather than emotionally fulfilling, the negative aspects of libido are at work. It would be better if partners understood the concept of "*albedo*." Albedo means white, but more technically it is the ratio of reflected light from a surface to the total light falling upon the surface. How is your *albedo*? How bright is your light?

Driving Force

For many there is confusion as to what is the driving force which pushes a relationship forward or the cohesive force which holds the relationship together. *Libido* is the instinct, the natural sexual urge which Western Civilization believes to be the glue which holds people together. Since it produces the passion that brings the opposite sexes together, it is falsely given credit for holding people together. *Libido* has more to do with procreation that it does with relationship. Sexual responses are important to a marriage relationship, a couple could not fulfill the purpose of the union without this function, but it must not be seen as central or a controlling aspect of the relationship. There must be more than sex. If *libido* is factored into the mastermind theory of relationship maintenance, it is doomed to fail. What is more important is the *albedo* of each of the partners. How does the reflected light of one affect the other?

Reflection of Light and Energy

Albedo literally means white and technically it is the rate of reflected light from a surface based on the total light falling upon that surface. For example, the earth's moon has no light of its own. What is seen is the reflected light, the *albedo*, of the sunlight as it is thrown back or returned toward the sun.

That is what is seen from the earth. The moon absorbs much of the light and only a small part is reflected back into the atmosphere.

The scripture informs the question that two believers walking together in God's light would reflect that light on each other and they would share *koninea*. This word is translated sharing, participation, communion, stewardship, in reality the concept of *koninea* points to participating in something in which others also participates or fellowship. It describes a kind of mutual involvement or participation in the light of God. Remember light is the absence of darkness just as health is the absence of disease. As this light is reflected, based on the total light received, one's *albedo* is either dull or bright. It is my firm conviction that the level of one's *albedo*, the reflected light of God as it shines on a partner, is more important than the level of one's *libido*.

What does this mean? God created sex with a dual function: (1) first, there is pleasure from the intimacy and the closeness opens the way for better understanding of the needs and desires of another; (2) second, the natural after glow of a sexual union is procreation. In fact, procreation is the reason for the pleasure. This is God's built-in assurance that the human race will produce offspring and endure to produce a family and complete the command "be fruitful and replenish the earth."

Refraction of Light

Refraction is this bending of a ray of light or energy as it passes indirectly from one channel to another of different concentration in which its speed is different or through layers of different concentration in the same channel. Sexual expression must not be an end in itself. Sex must not be the only interaction of a married couple. A sexual union is a kind of refraction of light and energy that may produce one of two end results: (1) a conception of a fetus that develops into a child for which the parents have continuing and long-term responsibility; or (2) the formation of new elements of a relationship that ensures continuing care and concern for a partner's well-being and the durability of the relationship.

Dual-purpose Process

When there is no bonding in sexual union, the dual-purpose of the process is thwarted. If the pleasure of sex outweighs the procreative aspect of the interaction, then the mindset must be adjusted to realize sex is not only an act; it is a self-perpetuating event that produces positive or negative consequences for a relationship. Procreation is an argument in favor of creating a future in which a couple cannot only combine their gene pools, but the two can work together and enjoy the upbringing of an offspring which is a result of their union. In other words, whether or not a sexual union produces an offspring, it must create something. Sex is only part of the maintenance of a marriage relationship. The sexual attraction becomes the glue that keeps the couple together so they can have a future.

The Future

Sex is not about the moment; it is about the future. Sexual expression should produce a positive consequence that relates to the longevity of the relationship. Permanence and durability are goals in a relationship. If sexual union produces a child then it obligates the parents to stick together and bring up the child in an ethical and moral manner. If the union does not produce a child, the sex act must still produce more than physical satisfaction; it should produce a lasting result that enables the relationship to have a future. In other words one sexual act could produce a child that the couple shares the nine months of development and the two decades of growing to maturity. If the act does not produce a conception, it should produce the beginning of closer ties and more beneficial relationship that will last for decades. Regardless of the outcome, sex relates to the future of a relationship not to the physical act. Should the reader assume this sounds a bit dichotomous; it is. My background, as a theologian and an educator, speaks to both aspects of the sexual relationship; (1) the building of a closer more intimate relationship and (2) the production of children to create a family. Both involve the future of the relationship.

Warning Signs of Troubled Relationship

Keeping separate agendas and/or calendars can create relationship problems. When one makes a schedule without considering what the other may be doing, trouble is brewing. It is easy to put many things above the marriage relationships: careers, children, hobbies, church, or community service. Couples should use the same working calendar to "pencil" in dates and events then periodically discuss the calendar together before the dates are transferred to the Master Calendar. Log data about both schedules on the final calendar, so each one knows where the other is and what they are doing, and that the event or "time apart" was agreed upon.

Putting a negative spin on actions and events is a sure sign of trouble in a relationship. A mature relationship requires giving each partner the benefit of the doubt. Motives should not be questioned. And there should never be the need for a "Second Story." The second story idea comes from a man who told a friend that he was a "Second Story Husband." When asked for an explanation, he simply explained, "If my wife doesn't believe the first story, I tell her a second one." Being late for dinner or other family activities can put pressure on a relationship. For this reason each member of a relationship must keep the other informed as to their schedule. It is true that "Love hides a multitude of sins" but there seems to be a "three strike rule" in effect here. Be careful. Accidents do happen, sometime one must work late at the office, etc. but with cell phones, I Pods, and e-mail there are no reasons for a partner to be kept in the dark about any necessary delay in schedule. If a partner is allowed to put a negative spin on the actions of the other partner, the seeds of a broken relationship are planted. The next time these seeds are watered, and then they grow and grow.

Reconciliation is Necessary

Reconciliation requires movement on the part of both partners. Neither can the variant behavior continue nor should a one-time incident be held against the partner in perpetuity when there is genuine regret and penitence. Some call reconciliation the sacrament of penance whereby wrongdoing is absolved through confession and penance. **Warning!** Never confess sexual misconduct to a mate; they may forgive, but they will never forget. Work on the antecedent causes with your partner and confess sins only to God. What was neglected? Who interfered? Why were you alone or away from your mate? God alone can forgive and forget (and never remember it against you again.) To err is human; to forgive is divine. Both parties should work on the causes of the improper behavior and move toward a permanent settlement of the issue. Come to an understanding and reach a ceasefire and do your first works over. Put a little courting back in the relationship. Only then can a couple be brought together for complete reconciliation. If one neglected and the other behaved improperly are not both guilty of something? Perhaps one would be more understanding if they clearly understood the power of the sexual urge. It is second only to the drive for self-preservation. True reconciliation will utilize the desire to preserve the relationship.

Relationships are Transitional

All relationships are transitional; all relationships are changing over time. Unless one recognizes these factors, dissatisfaction will result from a brief and isolated period in life and affect the whole of the relationship. This can be overcome by viewing life and relationships in a holistic manner. This means that periods or stages of all relationships must be viewed in the light of an integrated whole. It is clear from holism that the totality of a relationship has more value and worth that any specific period or stage of the relationship. Change is the one certain factor in all relationships. The consciousness that "this too shall pass" when difficulties are present is the glue that brings cohesion in a relationship with another. When things are great, one must also realize that any stage of a relationship cannot last forever. Change is both the constant that permits steady perseverance through times of trouble, and the common sense that enables one to enjoy the present moment is realizing that relationship is a journey. Look for flowers along the path and watch the birds and the bees.

Relationships are Dynamic

Relationships are dynamic; they have a driving force. There is a purpose which prompts the initial approach and a motivation that sustains the original proximity. A relationship is power in motion with a tendency toward change. Motives and controlling forces exist, both physical and moral, which manage action toward change. When one fails to clearly understand these motives and forces, change will both frighten the participants and disturb the relationship.

T-I-M-E and Change

A relationship needs space and time to work. The best spelling of love is t-i-m-e. God invented both love and t-i-m-e to provide opportunity for change. Change is an essential part of life, and real love makes it work. Change is the one thing that is certain in a relationship. Nothing can remain the same. What changes do you want made in your relationship? Exactly what change do you want your partner to make? Spell it out in writing before you discuss it with your mate. Don't just talk off the cuff. Remember the word spontaneous is associated with the word "combustion." An impromptu or impulsive statement about another's faults can gender a "back at you" squabble. Give your partner an equal opportunity to spell out the changes he/she expects you to make. This is both necessary and evenhanded. Do not permit such an exchange to become a "tit for tat" encounter. The list following begins with "him;" this is not to suggest the problems in marriage are gender based. As people mature they desire change in a relationship. It is better to make changes in behavior desired by your mate than to change partners. Marriage is a formal dance using only a "no break card" where no one is allowed to "cut in." The old adage "out of the frying pan; into the fire" is not an adequate solution.

What I want him to change:

1____

2____

3____

What I want her to change:

1. ____
____
____
____
____
____

2. ____
____
____
____
____
____

3. ____
____
____
____
____
____
____

Change is an essential aspect of all relationships.

Chapter Ten

The Touchstone Effect

Changes are Necessary

Nothing stays the same. Change exists in all relationships. How one deals with the changes determines the nature of the journey. The solution of problems is a necessary part of a permanent relationship. Sufficient to each day are the disappointments and discouragements, and these must not be allowed to accumulate. Never put off until tomorrow what should be done today. It will fester and your attitude will be worse tomorrow. If it happens today, if possible, fix it today. Do not permit the evening shadows to darken the situation. Usually one feels better in the daylight and the benchmarks established to guide the relationship are more evident and difficulties can be handled before darkness comes when both are tired.

A Precursor to Change

Change will come but all change should be evaluated against standard benchmarks established before the events occur. A touchstone was a black stone used to test the purity of gold and silver according to the color of the streak left when the metal was rubbed against it. When one assesses the nature and direction of change, it has a touchstone effect. When certain events occur or incidents happen in a relationship, they may become a precursor to constructive change.

The modification of behavior always has an antecedent cause that triggered the movement in either a positive or negative direction. It is helpful in maintaining a mature relationship that one learns the triggers or buttons that prompt a drastic response from another person. It appears that those who actually love each other can easily wound the other person often without realizing how it happened. This is why one should understand the reference points against which the quality of a relationship may be assessed. An honest and healthy relationship between spouses requires several things. The essential ingredients of an enduring relationship include touching, respect, heart-to-heart conversation, exclusivity, and a memory of endearing moments.

When Touching Stops

When **touching** stops the marriage is in trouble. There is a natural skin hunger in human beings. When the touching stops, the trouble begins. Individuals want to touch and be touched. If for any reason this is interrupted, one may seek to fulfill the skin hunger from "touching" someone else...or at least the partner will think so. Couples must enter joyfully into solving the skin hunger of a partner. If not, avoidance enters the picture and the touching stops.

When **respect** (to look at, and pay attention to) disappears, the exchange of a positive message wanes. At the first warning signal, action must be taken to repair the breach or the relationship will die sometimes slowly at other times rapidly. The warning signal is a time of crisis, but crisis also presents opportunities. Every cloud has a silver lining. One must learn that even the best marriages are similar to the weather. Cloudy days will come and the bright sunlight of respect loses its glow. Halos do rust and people do change. A new situation may call for new and drastic action. Each couple must find a simple plan of action when the opportunity presents itself. An equal mixture of love and respect makes a quality spousal glue to assist the cleaving required in a relationship.

When **heart-to-heart communication** becomes routine or ceases, the marriage becomes vulnerable. The partner must feel comfortable interrupting a favorite TV program, the morning newspaper, chores or even a shower with an interesting story, a joyful experience that must be shared, or a new joke that can't wait. Without the freedom to interrupt, a partner will soon lose interest. Serious trouble is near when a partner no longer understands the other's likes and dislikes or has forgotten those things that make the partner agitated or restless.

If the **promise of exclusivity** is broken, the marriage partner becomes angry, hurt and resentful. If the relationship sours, a "trump card" that was held in reserve may appear. The "trump card" may be a local Trollope or a new squeeze, but it spells "t-r-o-u-b-l-e" for the marriage. A third party added to the marriage mix creates an angry and aggrieved partner. When betrayal is revealed and irreconcilable differences develop, an explosion of violent feelings erupts and the marriage is sundered. The marriage pledge received as a token of love is a valued commodity and can withstand almost anything but stupidity and infidelity.

Should the **memory of endearing moments** fade, sarcasm begins. This is the use of cutting language that means the opposite of what they seem and are intended to ridicule. Becoming sarcastic about the way a couple met is often a first touchstone of trouble. It may mean that the excitement of early romance has been stepped on by another agenda. When the memories of the early romance are no longer sacred, the couple has begun to lose a hold on their relationship. Other troubles normally surface soon that often deal with money. Becoming bitter about the use of money can corrupt the whole of their cleaving. If one were to feel tricked, trapped, or even teased about the early days, the seeds of trouble are sprouting.

Failures and Positive Benefits

Failures and clouds of trouble often have positive benefits. First, be realistic, no one is perfect. No one can keep a partner totally informed on every activity of the day, but main events and activities that affect the partners schedule should be known by the other. No relationship is completely mature. There is room for daily growth. This does not justify a negative spin on actions and events unless it is part of a pattern. Sometimes a partner is sick; at other times individuals have "things on their minds" and need space and time to work through difficulties that have little to do with the relationship directly. Most of such areas of concern relate to health, work, extended family, money or the problems of others. Each one must be sensitive to a partner's needs. Remember, a burden shared is half as heavy. When these times come, there are several positive steps one can take.

Demonstrate a caring attitude. Do not challenge or give ultimatums. Introduce your concern in a soft voice. Be polite and respectful. An attitude is a predisposition to act. Each partner must demonstrate a positive attitude with a willingness to understand the relevant issues. A soft answer may save the day or at least open a way forward in the relationship.

Do not delay such an encounter. The longer one waits to speak up the more the situation festers and the tone of the voices become harder to control. Sacred writings clearly taught that "One should never let the sun go down on their wrath. Also, that each day has its own trouble and one should not permit them to accumulate. To wait is to compound the problem and to create an even more difficult situation. Visiting an uncle one Holiday Season as a child, I learned a good lesson. My uncle and aunt had some words and he went outside and sat backwards in an old chair under a shade tree. As the evening grew late he was heard to say, "Edith, it's getting dark!" He wanted to come in and reconcile the differences before the sun went down. This lesson has been remembered many times and used to mend the fence where the cow got out. Have you noticed that the cow usually gets out at the same place more than once?

Resolution requires flexibility. There are no easy solutions, only important choices. Love requires forgiveness and a predisposition to act reasonably. There must be a willingness to forgive or there can be no solution to relationship difficulties. Forgiveness must be spiritual, that is, forgiveness must include that the facts or the consequence of the event will not be remembered against the partner again. With such an attitude, there is hope for any relationship because this removes the shame of the "blame game" from the conversation and opens the door for proper communication.

Disappointed Partner

Partners have a right to be disappointed or even hurt when a partner violates sacred promises; however, one must be certain the violation is sufficient to dissolve the relationship or deal with it and then treat it as if it never happened. Instead of blame and dealing directly with the violation, one should look at the breach in relationship that precipitated the violation. Repair the breach and do not mess with the symptoms. With a mended relationship, a good partnership can move forward. For example, an adulterous spouse may be the symptom of a relationship difficulty rather that an overt act against the partner. Consequently, the concept of tough love makes clear that such acts are unacceptable in a good relationship, but the act or deed itself is bypassed to deal with the relationship problems which opened the door for the violation.

Unacceptable Behavior

This is not to justify such a violation, but to save a relationship one must be willing to understand the antecedent causes and deal with them in a mature and timely manner. Otherwise, the same issues will open the floodgates again. Did the couple spend enough time together; were they meeting the needs for intimacy; had the relationship deteriorate over time and the partners grew further and farther apart? Deal with these problems if you wish to save the relationship. Then make certain the offending party understands that this is a "one time offer" and should it happen again the consequences will be different. Although ultimatums are bad for a relationship because of the inherent moral weakness in humanity, it is necessary that an offending partner understand that certain behavior is unacceptable and must not continue. This must be clearly understood. Do not permit codependency issues to work against the necessary changes.

A-B-C of Relational Problems

When dealing with a relationship problem, the place to start is to look for an antecedent cause. Some happening or event before the behavior that may have been the stimulus that initiated it in the first place. **A**ntecedents push the **B**ehavior to occur. And the behavior is then strengthened or weakened by certain **C**onsequences following the behavior. Four categories of consequences follow a behavior and influence its cessation or continuance: there are both positive and negative reinforcement, punishment or ignoring. Whether the behavior ceases or gets stronger or weaker depends on the consequences. Negative behavior will continue if the consequences are weak. Also, strong positive consequences may reinforce the need for improved behavior. This is the best route to better relations with a spouse. Positive action may cancel negative behavior easier than any negative consequences. Any form of punishment or giving a "cold shoulder" will probably make things worse. Perhaps the old saying "One can trap more flies with honey than with vinegar" is true.

Negative Behavior

Why does negative behavior exist in a marriage? Apart from the fact that some folk are just inclined to misbehave (this should have been discovered during the dating period), there are many explanations for unacceptable behavior. Conceivably the person may not feel valued or may not have a sense of belonging. Experts on behavior know the result of such feelings and suggest there may be faulty logic involved in the negative thinking and behavior. At times it is possible to point out positive ways to meet this need; at other times it must be made clear that the negative behavior is unacceptable. Discuss the positive and the negative aspects of the problem and work with your partner to devise a plan to meet these needs in an appropriate way. Perhaps finding ways to value your partner and reinforce the sense of belonging could make a difference. If you value the partnership and feel a strong bond, make certain that your partner feels the connection and the affection. Regardless of what is done, make certain you demonstrate understanding.

Feelings of Inadequacy

Sometimes there are feelings of inadequacy underneath the bravado of seeking solace outside of marriage. Often there is deep need for comfort and consolation to overcome discouragement. If the partner feels rejected, they may arrive at "Why even try anymore?" This may cause a refusal to discuss the problem with anyone. So what does the offended party do? Work to develop a sense of belonging and *esprit de corp*. Make an effort to show your mate that you value them above all others. Never disparage the physical attributes of your mate. This is a ticket to trouble. Everyone has inadequacies but there are ways and means of compensating for most of these. At times a partner needs a small psychological boost, at other times medical attention may be the answer. Do something constructive and always be sensitive to the situation. Any negativity simply feeds the feeling of inadequacy. An unselfish and loving response is probably the best way forward. Common sense will guide you.

The Relationship Cycle

The basic problem in most relationships is that the individuals involved do not recognize that their association with others goes through cycles. Relationships are cyclical and move forward through time. When one feels dissatisfied with a particular stage of a relationship, it is often difficult for them to see the period as a part of a whole and that over time the situation will

CYCLE OF RELATIONSHIP

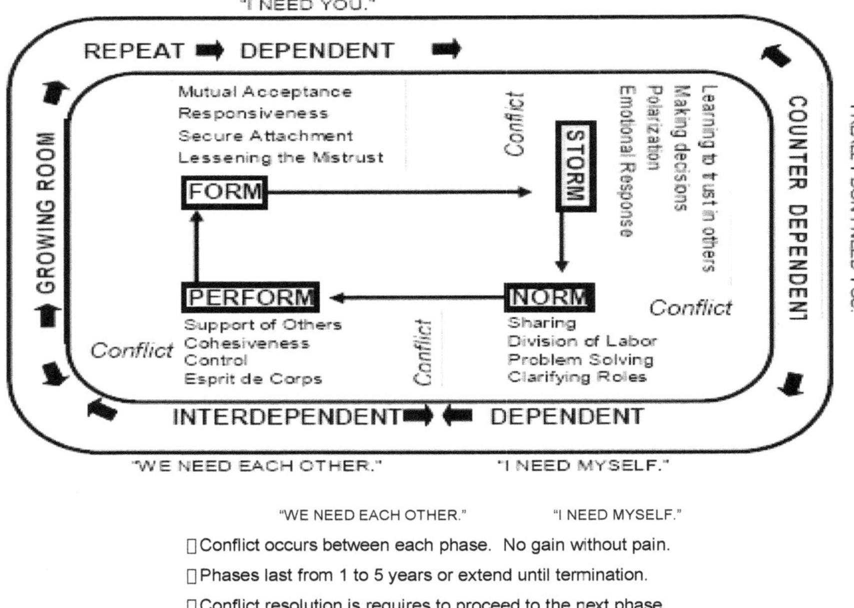

Figure 10.1 – Transition dynamics in marital relations.

change. This can be accomplished through a process called "transition dynamics." Provided one understands the stages of the process and selects the proper behavior, the transition from one phase to another will follow an acceptable pattern. Choosing a behavior that is inappropriate for a particular stage of a relationship will cause the matter to move in a negative direction. Material in other parts of this book will assist your understanding of the transition dynamics in force in the adjustment stages of marital relations.

Relationship Formula [n x (n-1) = R]

Transition dynamics attempts to explain the forces that produce activity and change in a relationship and bring to mind a realization that relationships are changed and modified at various periods of time. These phases or stages of change are called form, storm, norm and perform. Notwithstanding the material elsewhere in this book, an additional factor is the **relationship formula**. The number of people times the number of people minus one equals the number of interactive relationships in a group. [n x (n-1) = R].

Containment is the Issue

The higher the number of people involved the more difficult the solution to the problem. When a relationship goes sour, the number of people involved in attempting to fix the problem must be limited to a few trusted friends or one professional. For example a difficulty develops in a marriage and the couple (2) goes to their parents (4) and to their siblings (4) and involves their children (2) plus each partner's best friend (2) plus the clergy who performed the ceremony (1). The total number involved would be 2+4+4+2+2+1 = 15 people. When the relationship formula is applied the number 15 x the number 15-1 (15x14) = 210 interpersonal interactions. This means with only 15 people in the mix 210 interpersonal interactions are created not counting the people added through gossip each day. This so complicates the solution to a relationship problem that nothing is accomplished or the already problematic situation is made worse. When trouble comes and come it will, couples must limit the number of people who know about their difficulties. Containment is the issue if they wish to save the relationship.

Private Behavior and Public Scandal

One can easily see when private behavior becomes a "public scandal" there is little hope of fixing the relationship because of the exposure number. Even in a town with a population of 15,000 with a weekly newspaper, a radio station, and thousands gossiping over the backyard fence, on the telephone, or in the barbershops, the whole town knows about a crime or an affair; there is little chance of a fair trial for the criminal or a reasonable reconciliation for a marriage. Apply the formula: 15,000 times 14,999 equals 22,498,500 interpersonal interactions and reactions to a private problem. It is no wonder jury pools are tainted by the media. Although many feel that personal behavior does not impact the performance of public duties, the exposure of marital scandals by the national media almost negates a private solution to infidelity. The details are blasted on 24/7/365 news outlets and political enemies and "saints who have never been caught" compound the damages to the spouse, the children, and indirectly the general public. Is there any chance of living down an indiscretion when the whole world knows more than the spouse about the incident? Tragically. if the public gives the person a "pass" on the behavior it sends the wrong message to the young. What is the answer?

Morality and Ethics

Morality and ethics must be put back into the conscience of the general population. Respect for the sanctity of marriage must be restored. The private lives of people must be respected. The young must be taught the proper way to select a mate and behave in marriage. Without these changes there will simply be a progressive debauchery with morality and ethics absent from society. It appears that the world is repeating the excesses and depravity that destroyed ancient Rome. There has always been evil in the world since the Fall of Lucifer and the problem in the Garden of Eden, but in the past it has been contained to an area or region or confined to back streets of the old cities, but now it is in the public square, the corporate office, the political office, the classroom, the Internet, and it is destroying the moral and ethical fiber of the people.

The place to start is the valley of despair at the bottom of the Hill of Difficulty and proceed post haste to the summit for a meeting of the minds and determine ways and means of educating the young, preserving the integrity of private relationships, and protecting the sanctity of marriage. There will always be pockets of wickedness in the world, but it does not have to invade and destroy the family and the future of civilization. Both a public and a private agenda are required. The problems must be attacked on both fronts. After all, behavior is a personal and private action that affects the lives of individuals, the family, the community, the state, and the nations of the world. A good beginning would be to correct the excesses in the dating/mating game, reinforce the sanctity of the marriage vows, and preserve the two-parent "family" as the bedrock of society. The alternative is to live in "paradise lost" without civil constraints or private and public integrity. We must climb this Hill of Difficulty together.

**"We were on the same rope;
we got there together."**

Sir Edmund Hilary

Chapter Eleven

The Hill Of Difficulty

Climbing the Hill of Difficulty as a married couple is the first step in reaching the summit for a meeting about improving society. Putting first things first is a main concern. Throughout moral history the family has had priority. As various religions developed, they all valued the family as a key to progress in society.

The priority institutions are based on ordaining and ordering by Providence of three basic institutions, (1) a two-parent family, (2) a moral community, and (3) a faith-based environment. Each of these relate to the individual; the family **produces** individuals, the community **protects** individuals, and a faith-based environment **preserves** individuals in the context of both family and community. Keeping this priority is essential to a moral society. Understanding the priority of the family is a necessary part of a marriage relationship.

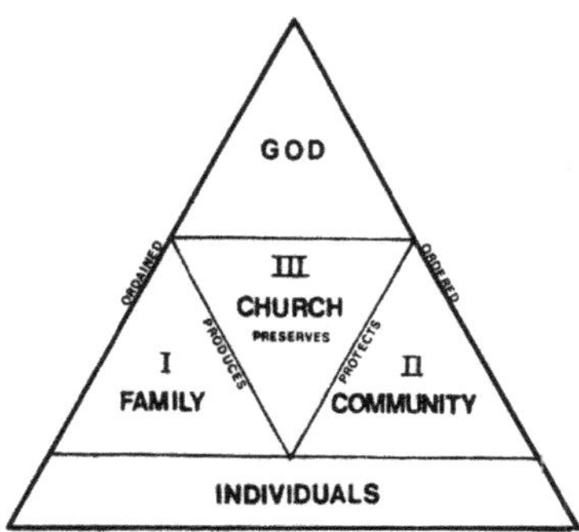

Figure 11.1 – Institutions related to the individual in priority order.

This is the difficult hill that must be climbed if the individual is to be honorably produced, honestly protected, and holistically preserved in the arena of morality and ethics by a faith-based entity. The individual must have priority in all aspects of a civilized society. If accomplished, the home would be adequate to nourish the child, the school would be sufficient to equip the student, and a faith-based entity would preserve the whole individual in a wholesome family, protect them in a livable community, and holistically prepare the individual for a moral and ethical journey into marriage, family building, community work, and productive social engagement in society. It is a difficult task, but it can be done provided the individual and the family have the historical priority both deserved and required for a moral society.

Climbing the Hill

John Bunyan's difficult struggle to continuing a service to the community while imprisoned is an example of spiritual achievement in an adverse and difficult environment. John Bunyan, an Englishman, wrote at least 50 books, but one stands out above all others; it was Pilgrim's Progress written in prison. Bunyan had strong convictions about his call to service and refused to permit the English government or the Church of England to endorse his credentials. He felt that a call from God was sufficient authorization to serve. For this conviction of independence he served twelve years as a prisoner in the Tower of London. During that period, with only a quill pen and paper, Bunyan wrote Pilgrim's Progress about a pilgrim's journey to the heavenly heights. His book outsold all other books in the English language with the exception of the English Bible.

A Fascinating Story

In documenting the progress of this traveler, Bunyan wrote a most fascinating story. In many respects the pilgrimage parallels the struggle of civil and marital problems. Such a venture is indeed "climbing the Hill of Difficulty." In Bunyan's story as the traveler struggled up the Hill of Difficulty, he met two frightened and nervous men running down hill. One was named Timorous and the other Fearful. As these nervous and frightened men passed, they yelled, "Don't go up there. There are lions up there!" The traveler, without hesitation, responded, "To go back is nothing but death, I will go forward!" This is the attitude that civil and marital problem solvers must possess.

When the traveler arrived at the summit of the Hill of Difficulty, he saw that lions were indeed there but he noticed they were chained with a short chain, and if he walked the "straight and narrow path" between them, the lions could not reach him. As he passed the lions he also noticed they were old, feeble, and their teeth were broken. He realized the "straight and narrow way" protected him from the intimidating lions. Citizens who are concerned about their community and the institution of marriage and choose to walk the ethical and moral path should not be threatened by the pitfalls or dangers on the journey up the Hill of Difficulty. They should approach the process with confidence that steady progress will go to those who persevere.

A realistic word! The journey and the struggle against injustice and immorality are difficult, but rewarding. It may be an uphill battle, but the end result will be rewarding. To know that you did your best is also a reward of the first order! Certainly there are predatory lions and lionesses along the way, individuals who wish to justify their own lives below moral standards by justifying those who violate traditional ethics and morality. Good moral conduct and a fervent prayer will chain and restrain the "lions" so they cannot reach you personally. For the sake of family values, one must walk the straight path and persevere. Walking this straight and narrow path is best done by a couple walking together.

The Plural Pronouns

To walk together there must be agreement. Personal and joint prayer is a powerful weapon in the fight to keep marriage on the right track. No one asked Jesus to teach them individually to pray, but the petition was "teach us" to pray as John taught his disciples. It is obvious that the response to the request was for the Master Teacher to emphasize the plural nature of the pronouns; us, our, and we

.

1. As Jesus ceased praying in a certain place, one of his disciples asked, Lord, teach **us** to pray, as John taught his disciples. 2. And Jesus said, When you pray say **Our** Father, may your name be honored. Your reign begin, your will be done in Heaven and on earth. 3. Continue giving **us** daily the food **we** need. 4. And forgive **our** sins; for **we** too forgive all who are indebted to **us**. And keep **us** clear of temptation, and rescue **us** from evil (Luke 11:1-4 DNT).

Hills and Valleys

There will be hills and valleys in every relationship. In fact the secret to longevity in a relationship is learning to cope with the ups and downs. It should be remembered that for every mountain top there is a valley both before and after.

Life is a rollercoaster ride in stormy weather. There will be scary times and fearful stops and starts. There will also be mountain top experiences that provide great happiness but one cannot develop a pesimestic attitude anticipating the valley that will come. My neice once said to my wife, "Don't feel bad because you don't feel good!" Learn to bank the happiness and spend it in the valley. In fact, while you are in the valley pick a few flowers and wade in the cool stream. This will prepare you for the climb to the mountain top. The highs and lows are tradeoffs, similar to altitude and speed in flying. My memory is clear how pleased it was to learn from a flight instructor that one could trade altitute for speed and speed for altitude. So the marital journey is a trade off. Enjoy the present moment on the mountain top, cautiously coast down and gather speed to cross the valley quickly and gather momentum to climp the next hill.

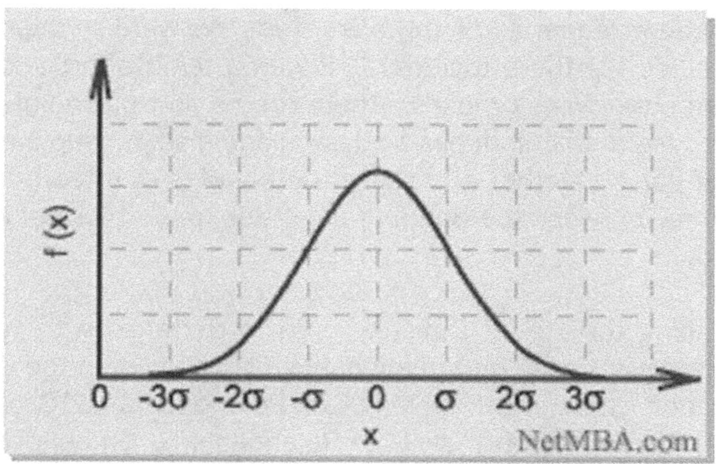

1/6 outside [2/3 inside] 1/6 outside

Figure 11.2 – The mountain climbing experience.

In applying mountain climbing to married life, they are both similar to the bell curve, where only one-third is in the valley, while two-thirds are either a rough climb to the top, enjoying the summit, or careful trip down the other side. It would be helpful if marriage partners learned some mountain climbing rules and practiced some of the saftey procedures necessary to stay alive on the steep slopes. If the behavior of each party to the marriage is understood from the prospecive of mountain climbing, a couple would find ample guidance for the journey. One major discovery would be that they are on the same rope and that the quality of the climb and even their very lives depend on each other. Mountain climbers refuse to lose ground when they are confronted by an obstacle that prevents upward or forward progress; they make a lateral move and search for a way up without losing altitute.

When Sir Edmund Hilary and Tenzing climbed Mt. Everest in 1953, and returned to the base camp, reporters asked "Who made it to the top first, Hilary or Tenzing? Who was the first man to set foot on top of the world?" Hilary spoke as the expediton leader and firmly answered, "We were on the same rope; we got there together." It was a team effort and the team either wins or loses. There are no first place finishers when life and limb depend on someone else. A couple reach their goals together and share the benefits of a team effort or they both lose the battle of the sexes to the tricks of a low bidder.

Climbing the Hill of Difficulty is in four stages with varing emphasis on task and relationship. (1) behavior in the valley preceding the climb (High Task/Low Relationship); (2) Climbing the mountain (High Task/High Relationship); (3) behavior at the summit (High Relationship/Low Task; and (4) Descending the opposite slope to the next valley (Low Relationship/Low Task). A couple encounters valleys and mountains as they journey toward eternity.

Valley - High Task/Low Relationship

In the **valley preceding the climb** up the Hill of Difficulty, the couple in preparation for the climb must maintain high task and low relationship. This a time to work and plan not play, and there is no time to stop and smell the flowers. The task at hand is to prepare for the climb by checking supplies and equipment. Halfway up the mountain there are no stores or shops to purchase what is needed; it must be anticipated, packed, and carried on the climb. In other words, the couple will be alone during this climb. Others may be supportive but the couple is climbing the hill unaided. This is their personal journey and they must both do the planning, preparation, and work together.

Climbing Up the Hill - High Task/High Relationship
When the climb begins up the mountain things change. Now the behavior is high task/ high relationship. Climbing the mountain the couple will be tied to the same rope and will assist each other in securing firm footing and the proper use of equipment. In fact, that is one of the lessons of mountain climbing, there is no outside assistance, a 911 call will not be answered, mama can't be reached on the phone; perhaps God is the only one listening. Each other is all you have. Life and fortune depend on each other. The behavior is high task/ high relationship. This is serious business; it is life or death.

Meeting at the Summit - High Relationship/Low Task
Behavior at the summit is a brief respite for a breather and a brief time to enjoy the view, take a brief rest and prepare for descending the opposite side of the mountain. Hopefully, while at the summit the couple can attend the meeting of community, state, and national leaders who are interested in the morality and ethics of the community and the quality and state of the two-parent home for the raising of children. The couple has a brief time to give their advice and consent relative to the issues involved and then they must proceed with the planned descent and their behavior in the next valley.

Traversing the Downside – Low Relationship/Low Task

Descending the dangerous opposite side of the mountain and crossing the next valley now becomes a priority. They have earned the rest and now have time to enjoy each other, have a summit meeting, and consider the dangerous downhill trek. As soon as they cross the next valley there will be another mountain to climb. Hopefully, they have picked up a little of the spirit of Joshua who when about to enter the Promised Land and knew of the giants and the walled cities that were to be formidable obstacles to possessing the land said, "Give me this mountain." Knowing the opposition and the difficulty of the task, Joshua embraced the task and asked for the location where the giants and the walled cities were. Joshua and Caleb made an affirmation in light of the difficulties and said, "We are well able to take it!" This is the attitude a couple must have to complete the journey and make it over the top to get ready for the next phase of the unfinished task.

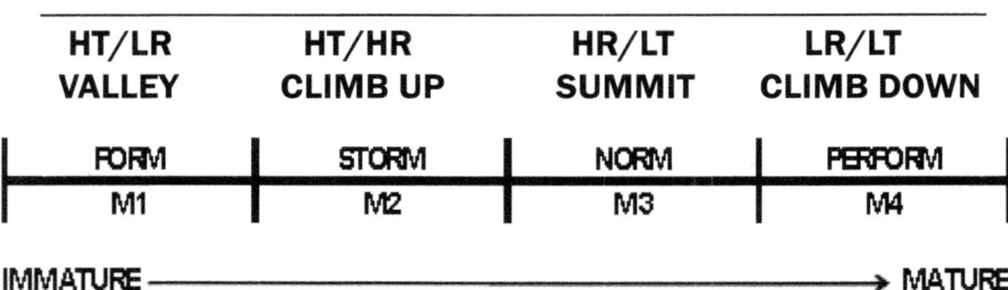

Figure 11.3 – Sequence for climbing the Hill of Difficulty.

Building a Relationship Team

The solemn pledge represented in the marriage vows are general guidelines for behavior of both spouses. Below is a paraphrasing of the original Ten Commandments that seemed to have a male orientation, but the commandments for marriage are not gender specific. They are directed to both parties relative to acceptable behavior to maintain personal integrity and moral uprightness in the marriage relationship.

The Ten Commandments of Marriage

1. **You must have no one else but me.**
2. **You must not keep mementos from past romances.**
3. **You must not worship any strange gods.**
4. **You must respect my name and my family.**
5. **You must both work and worship.**
6. **You must respect and support your parents.**
7. **You must not harbor hate for anyone.**
8. **You must not adulterate the marriage vows.**
9. **You must always tell the truth about the neighbors.**
10. **You must not desire a house beyond your means, or covet anything that belongs to your neighbor, including the neighbor's spouse.**

The worth of sentimental recollection
Should not be overlooked...

Chapter Twelve

The Empty Box

A Blank Slate

Marriage is a new beginning, a blank slate, upon which will be written a narrative of significant events in the lives of two people in love. When newlyweds come to the altar with "naught save love" and realize that marriage is an Empty Box which they have the privilege of filling with their own "stuff." The box becomes their own "book of remembrances" as they add to it daily, weekly, monthly, and yearly. Here are some of the substantial things that will overflow that Empty Box:

1. **Companionship** as they become strong together.
2. **Friendship** as they build a compatible relationship.
3. **Intimacy** which is more than sex, but less than possession.
4. **Affection** without total gratification, but ultimate achievement
5. **Security** based on long-term commitment and care.
6. **Partnership** as they work to achieve common goals.
7. **Completion** both personal and social as they build a family.

A Treasure Chest or an Empty Box

Marriage may be seen as a Treasure Chest filled with valuables simply for the taking. Some marry for wealth others for security, but all marry for the anticipated benefits the experience should bring. When in fact the individual they marry should be regarded as a person of worth and value and that this personal treasure would appreciate in value over time. It should be remembered that both personal property and people appreciate in value. As the marriage relationship grows there are many meaningful memories that should be valued. The worth of sentimental recollection should not be overlooked because these memories have value that increases over time.

Similar to a young lady's Hope Chest filled with accumulated items for use after her wedding, marriage is an empty box in which to store the most personal of intimate memories of a relationship. This box filled with affection and a stock of retained knowledge and experience cannot be purchased, rented, or borrowed; it must be accumulated and valued over time. The treasure of memories in this box can assist a couple over the course of the journey and keep hope alive and love working to the advantage of a lasting relationship. Learning to value a partner and a partnership is part of what holds a marriage together.

Unreasonable Expectation

Today's youth have unreasonable expectations. They expect to have on their wedding day all the accumulated property and assets that took their parents 20 to 30 years to acquire. They have been on a Treasure Hunt and expect marriage to provide a Treasure Chest of goodies that will make them instantly wealthy. Parents do their children a disservice when they provide them with everything they need and want, and they never get the privilege of buying a new car, furnishing a new home, decorating a baby's room, or purchasing affordable gifts for their children. Grandparents can be so unwise; such as, buying a bicycle for a three-month old boy or giving a pony as a gift to a one-year old girl. What happened to wisdom? What happened to letting the young couple stand on their own four-feet?

The Means to Live Beyond

Easy credit and the free gifts of parents and friends cause a couple to live beyond their means. Things a couple cannot afford for themselves; they should not have. The first lesson of marriage is to learn to live within one's means. The little ones who come into this family must also learn to live within the means of their parents. Surely everyone wants the best for their children and grandchildren, but what are the lessons learned from overindulgence? Bitter seeds are being sown that will spring up in a bitter tree with bitter fruit during marriage. No wonder the new generation behaves as if they have eaten sour grapes. When personal happiness is based on material things, there is little hope of building permanence in a relationship. When personal satisfaction is the goal of a relationship, there will be certain disappointment.

Experience the Struggle

Marriage is not a treasure hunt on a distant sea shore; it is an Empty Box at the altar waiting to be filled with the affection and affordable things plus many meaningful memories. Since medical records show that birth by C-Section takes about five (5) years off the life of a child, probably because the infant did not experience the struggle of the birth canal, what does the "easy start" and the "living beyond their means" bring to the marriage relationship? Perhaps, without the personal struggle of new beginnings and first things, a young couple does not develop the toughness needed to survive the sure struggles of human relationships. Why rob the newlyweds of the delight and pleasure of moving from a rented apartment to a new home or driving an old car until funds are available for a new one. Part of the strength of marriage is that two people can struggle together and overcome most difficulties. Spiritual arithmetic points out that "two are better than one." For generations the strength of two working together has been sufficient to build a home, grow a family, and live out their lives in peace and harmony. What about the beauty of love combined with "the bare necessities" that precipitates a conversation similar to this:

Come walk with me; the best is yet to be.
The future will be better than the past.
Together we can make it last.
And when we make a home,
It will be ours alone!

One must remember that marriage is finding a mate for the rest of your life. Those who take the vows of marriage are brought into the closest and most sacred of human relationships. Their lives are blended into one as the waters of confluent streams are mingled, and thenceforth, they must share the joys and sorrows of life. And from this close and intimate relationship spring obligations of the most solemn and lasting character. With marriage a couple begins life under new conditions and with larger responsibilities; and it is only by faithfully performing the duties and fulfilling the obligations of the new relationship that true and lasting happiness can be found.

Marriage is Like a Mountain Railway

There are two kinds of rail systems, the light rail system that uses light- weight equipment and operates in a limited area and the heavy rail system that accommodates larger equipment and larger loads and goes to more places. The dating relationship could be compared to the light rail system while married life is more akin to the heavy rail system.

A marriage relationship is similar to the construction of a railroad through a mountain range with steep slopes, deep valleys and unstable soil. It is possible, but will not be easy. There is one track and one train. The box cars are empty and will be loaded with personal "marriage stuff." The engine, the cars and the track and roadbed must have regular maintenance to insure a train reaches the intended destination.

++

ONE TRAIN - ONE RELATIONSHIP - TWO TRACKS – HELD TOGETHER BY CROSSTIES AND REGULAR MAINTENANCE

++

There are two tracks which are kept equal distance apart by crossties. If the tracks narrow or get too close together there is trouble for the train. Should the tracks get too far apart, there is trouble for the train. The railway is laid on a bed of rocks which must be tended carefully to support the track and the train. Neglect of any aspect of the roadbed and disaster is coming down the track. Crossties are supports placed between the double rails to strengthen the rails and hold the tracks together. The crossties are critical to the construction and maintenance of the railroad and are placed crosswise to give strength and support for the rails. These transverse timbers supporting the rails of a railroad track are required to keep the rails straight and an equal distance apart. The crossties are similar to the relationship work necessary to keep a marriage on track and safely operating. Placing new crossties is part of the perpetual maintenance.

The rails are directional. They run away from one direction and toward another. The train always appears to go forward, but it depends on the destination as to which way is forward. A train going back to Chicago would appear to be going forward and a train going to New York City would also appear to move forward. It is a matter of perception. Relationships are always moving, they are dynamic and at times it is difficult to know if they are headed in the right direction.

Tracks are made of rails usually fastened to wood ties and designed to carry the weight of a locomotive and boxcars attached to the train. A railway system creates a network between buildings, cities, and functions as a transport system to carry people and goods and services without loss or waste. When trouble comes, the usual question asked "Is this any way to run a railroad?" The same could be asked of a dysfunctional marriage relationship. "Is this any way to make a marriage work?"

CHANGE HAS TAKEN PLACE AND THE MARRIAGE VOWS MUST BE RENEGOTIATED.

Affirmation of the Marriage Vows

We are met in the presence of God to affirm the marriage vows of **JOHN** and **JANE**. The husband is under obligation to protect his wife, to shield her from the rough storms of the world, to cling to her with unfaltering fidelity, to cherish her with unfailing affections, and to guard her happiness with unceasing vigilance. And the wife is under obligation to love and cherish her husband, to honor and sustain him, and to be true to him in all ways. This love of which I speak is slow to lose patience--it looks for a way of being constructive. It is not possessive: it is neither anxious to impress nor does it cherish inflated ideas of its own importance. Love has good manners and does not pursue selfish advantage. It is not touchy. It does not compile statistics of evil or gloat over the wickedness of other people. On the contrary, it is glad with all good men when Truth prevails. Love knows no limit to its endurance, no end to its trust, no fading of its hope; it can outlast anything. It is, in fact, the one thing that still stands when all else has fallen. Each one is under obligation to fulfill the love ordained of God and recorded in I Corinthians 13:1-13 (DNT)

1. Even if I could speak the languages of men and angels and not have love, I would become an echoing gong or a clanging cymbal. 2. Even if I have the gift of speaking forth God's word, and understand sacred secrets, and all knowledge; and though I have absolute faith and be able to move mountains, and have not love, I am nothing. 3. And though I distribute all I possess to provide for the poor, and though I seal my witness at a burning stake, and have not love, there is no benefit for me. 4. Love is longsuffering and sympathetic; love has no jealousy, love is not anxious to impress others, does not hold inflated ideas of self-importance, 5. Has good manners, is not self-seeking, is never provoked, does not keep score of wrongs; 6. takes no pleasure in wrongdoing, but rejoices when truth is victorious; 7. There is no limit to endurance, love has endless faith and great expectations, there is no end to love's tolerance. 8. Love stands when all else disintegrates: but preaching, the use of unnaturally acquired languages and present and fragmentary knowledge will be rendered entirely idle. 9. For we presently speak based on limited knowledge. 10. But when Christ returns, then our limited function will become inoperative. 11. When I was a child, I spoke, understood, and reasoned as a child: but becoming a man, I outgrew childish ways. 12. At the present we see only blurred reflections in polished metal; but then face to face the blurred image will be gone and we will see ourselves as God sees us. 13. Now there are three things that endure forever: faith, hope, and love; but the greatest of these is love. (DNT)

And now, if you, knowing of nothing either legal or moral to forbid your continued union in marriage, wish to reaffirm your vows and assume the full obligations marriage, indicate that wish by **joining your right hands.**

JOHN, do you now freely take, **JANE**, whose hand you hold to be your wedded wife, and solemnly promise and reaffirm your vows to her and pledge to loyally fulfill your obligations as her husband to protect her, honor her, love her, and cherish her in adversity as well as in prosperity and keep yourself unto her alone, so long as you both shall live? ***The man shall answer*: I will.**

JANE, do you freely reaffirm your marriage vows, and accept this man, **JOHN**, whose hand you hold to be your wedded husband and solemnly promise that you will be unto him a tender, loving, and true wife through sunshine and shadow alike, and be faithful to him as long as you both shall live? ***The woman will answer*: I will.**

Then shall they loose their hands: We read in an old story that when God made a covenant with Noah, He set a bow in the cloud as a token of remembrance, and said, "I will look upon it, that I may remember the everlasting covenant." From this we learn that it is well for us, when we enter into solemn agreement one with another, to set apart some reminder of what we have promised. As tokens of your marriage covenant, you have each selected a wedding ring.

Here the ring(s) shall be given to the minister*:* A chosen wedding ring fittingly represents the valued ties that unite husband and wife. These rings, endless until broken by outside forces, are fit symbols of the unbroken partnership of marriage which should continue until broken by death. Let them be unto you constant reminders of your obligations to each other, and mute incentives to their fulfillment.

Forasmuch as the husband imparts to his wife his name and receives her into his care and keeping, I give you this ring. Put it upon the wedding finger of your companion, and say to her these words: I, **JOHN,** give this ring to you, **JANE,** and by this act declare, in the presence of these witnesses, that I reaffirm my marriage vows to you and take you to be my beloved wife; that I will be unto you a faithful husband until death shall part us.

Take the ring which you have selected, put it upon the wedding finger of your companion and say to him these words: I, **JANE,** give this ring to you, **JOHN,** and thus declare, in the presence of these witnesses that you are the husband of my choice, that I will be faithful to you until death shall part us.

As you both wear wedding rings, they become a symbol of the perfect circle of duty that makes you one. As you hope for happiness in your married life, I charge you to be true to the vows you have taken. With your marriage, you begin life under new conditions and with larger responsibilities; and it is only by faithfully performing the duties and fulfilling the obligations of this new relationship that true and lasting happiness can be found.

Since, **JOHN** and **JANE** have openly declared their wishes to reaffirm their marriage vows and continue their legal marriage and pledged love and fidelity each to the other, and have confirmed the same by the giving and receiving of a ring, I, as a Minister of the Gospel, pronounce that they continue to be Husband and Wife. (*Torches, candles, or salt may be used here***!)**

Would you look at each other and repeat: Entreat me not to leave you or to return from following you; for where you go I will go, and where you lodge I will lodge; your people shall be my people, and your God my God (Ruth 1:16).

Let us pray: Almighty God, heavenly Father of mankind, whose nature is love: Look with favor upon this man and this woman who have taken fresh vows before you. Grant this to be more than an outward union, but rather the blending of hearts and spirits. Bless each with the inward qualities of loyalty, self-control, trust, cooperation, and forgiveness, that they may keep faithfully this holy covenant, and may live together all their days in true love and perfect peace, through Jesus Christ. **The Lord bless you and keep you; the Lord make His face to shine upon you, and be gracious unto you; the Lord lift up His countenance upon you and give you peace. Amen.**

JOHN and **JANE** you may now seal your love and commitment with a kiss! Ladies and gentlemen: May I introduce a new and refreshed Mr. and Mrs. **JOHN DOE.**

The Reverend Hollis L. Green, ThD, PhD

____DATE

MAN

____DATE

WOMAN

A GOOD MARRIAGE REQUIRES
AN UPDATED CONTRACT.

Appendix A

Lyrics of Songs by Hollis to Gail

Through the years I have written lyrics and sung them to Gail. In response, she wrote prose and read to me.

This has been an ongoing experience. Here are excerpts from Love's Conversation....it continues and is good!

"Sweet Talker"

Based on a conversation Gail had with her mother.

One day I sat my daughter down
And said please don't frown.
I must tell you about men.
Some are Smooth Talkers;
Some are Sweet Talkers.
And some don't talk at all,
But they all have a line.

I looked up at her so sad,
And said, Mama please don't be mad
But I just can't handle it by myself.
I need a Smooth Talker.
I want a Sweet Talker.
And if the man can't talk at all,
I'll do the talking myself
I just can't make it by myself.

"One Little Word"

This tune was written after a serious conversation.

One little word
Made me happy.
One little word
Made me grin.
One little word
From a special person:
That one word was "When."

She said,
"When we get married,
I'll be good to you."
She said,
"When we get married,
I'll always be true."

So, one little word
Made me happy.
One little word
Made me grin.
One little word
From a special person:
That one word was "When."

"I'd Give a Dollar for You!"

Knowing I was a poor man by most people's calculations, I penned this little jingle

I'd give a nickel for an apple
And a tangerine;
A dime for a coke and a magazine,
A quarter for a lady
And a limousine.
But I'd give a dollar for you!

Got no money, got no fame.
Just one dollar to my shame.
All I have is my good name,
But I'd give a dollar for you!

Lady, I know you are not for sale.
My Love for you could put me in Jail.
There's no one to go my bail,
But I'd give a dollar for you!

Lady, If your love is free.
Simply smile back at me.
We'll take the dollar--start a family.
I pledge my love to you.

I'd give a nickel for an apple
And a tangerine;
A dime for a coke and a magazine,
A quarter for a lady
And a limousine.
But I'd give a dollar for you!

"My Heart Beats For You"

During a long absence overseas,
I wrote the words to this tune.

It's been a long, long day
And you are miles away,
But my heart beats for you!
The evening is near
And you are not here,
But my heart beats for you.

When I think and think of you
And remember how true your
Heart has been through the years
With each heartache and tear
You were there to cheer,
And my heart beats for you – dear!

"It's Nice to be Home with You"

Home after a long trip, one morning these words
came pouring out of my heart.

It's nice to be home in the evening
Home with the one I love.
To talk about life and living
And plan the future with love.

It's nice to be home in the morning,
Wake up by the one you love.
To smell the fresh brew
Read a paper for two,
It's nice to be home with you!

"You March at the Head of My Band"

After dreaming about us and our relationship, these words were put on paper for Gail

You march at the head of my band.
My heart beats a melody
I don't understand.
But this one thing is true,
I'll always love you.
You march at the head of my band.

Every day you march through my memory.
Every night you parade through my dreams.
Your love holds the key,
To my life's harmony.
Without you how lost I would be.

You march at the head of my band.
My heart beats a melody I don't understand.
But this one thing is true,
I'll always love you.
You march at the head of my band.

Appendix B

Prose Written by Gail to Hollis

My mother loved Gail and appreciated the home she made for me and the boys. Gail wrote this poem as a tribute to her, Grace Curtin Green.

Mother

Mother -
She was a lady.
Head held high,
Yet not so much
She could not see
The need of her only son.

No restrictions placed on him -
Released to live life as best he could.
How proud she was of her boy,
Just pure, unadulterated love.

She was a comfort
- Grace -
A fitting name don't you think?

Because of You

Written as a Father's Day gift

Because of you,
I have experienced things
Which otherwise
Would be closed to me:
A girl's tender years;
A toddler's innocent activity;
A boy's loving embrace.

Because of you,
The world of children
Is also my world -
Things I could only dream of
You have opened to me.

Because of you,
I have experienced a semblance
Of the ecstasy and agony
Of being a parent - bittersweet -
Although the range of my emotions
Could not possibly reach
The height or depth of yours.

I am not called mother,
But motherhood Is a part of me -
Because of you.

The Seasons Change

The seasons change -
Summer is here.
Where did spring go
Or winter for that matter?
Twenty-two years of being your wife -
The time has flown; good times, bad times,
We've weathered them together.
Hopes flair, hearts rise to meet the New Year,
Then, in an instant the next one is here.

This has been a year of change -no matter!
There's no need to fret.
God knows, yes, He knows,
We are not alone in this endeavor.

Time marches on, people come and go.
Transition, alternation,
It goes on and on.

Yet, something never alters; we can always rely.
Like its Maker, ever faithful,
Set in motion for our time -
The seasons change.

I Watch You

I watch you -
As you create things.
Your many talents surprise me:
Painting a picture;
Making an old piece of furniture come to life;
Making our house into a home

I watch you -
As you think of ways to help people.
Your mind runs so fast
With ideas sent from the heavenlies.
So much to accomplish in so little time.

I watch you -
As you work.
Work so hard you are at the point of exhaustion.
Frustrated at so much to be done,
You work against high odds:
Limited resources,
People's unrealistic expectations,
And your own humanity.
Yet - you never stop working,
Never stop hoping,
Never stop doing your part.

I watch you -
As you deliver a sermon from your very soul.
Providence interceding with humanity -
The anointed of God.

I watch you -
As you teach others what you have been taught.
A spiritual legacy from your father, Barton;
Wisdom from Grandfather Green; unconditional
Love and support from your Grandmother Green;
Patient discipline from your mother, Grace.

I am ever learning -
Because I watch you!

Saturday Morning

It's Saturday morning, peaceful and calm.
Reading the newspaper, drinking coffee -
No hurry - sublime.
Knowing we have the whole day together feels good.

We move about the house in harmony as in a dance.
Coffee in the chairs by the sunlit windows,
Breakfast at the table under the rhythmic fan.
You move to the desk to edit your written word,
I sit at the table pen and paper in hand.
Separate rooms, but together.

A sigh of contentment -
I can hear your fingers moving across the keys.
It seems getting the words out of your mind
And onto paper is so important now.
We sense the speeding passage of time.

I look out the window.
The sky is blue, the grass is green, the sun is bright.
Experiencing the present moment,
My memory recalls an anonymous quote,
"My past is redeemed, the present makes sense,
My future is secure."
In God's hands I feel complete.

The last day of the week, the Sabbath,
We wind down in preparation for the new week
Which promises so much activity.
Responsibility interrupts my pleasant thoughts -
Groceries to buy, clothes to launder, bills to pay -
It's OK.
How grateful I am that these basic things
Can be accomplished.
Enveloped by the Spirit of God
The seesaw of a well ordered life
Moves between sublime and mundane.

What should I do next? Launder the clothes,
Buy the groceries, weed the garden?
I don't think so.
It's Saturday morning -
No hurry - the flowers are so beautiful -
Ahhh

A Simple Gesture

As I drove away,
You blew me a kiss.
A simple gesture,
Yet, so full of meaning.
Thank you, I love you it said.

Being together is more important, now.
It seems we savor the companionship -
Love and friendship intertwined.
We sat in the gazebo to rest. A cool breeze,
Cold water to drink -
Simple pleasures for two.

That slight movement of your hand -
It made the trip worthwhile.
Thank you, I love you,
my friend.

I Missed You

I missed you -
You were gone from my sight
But not from my heart.

I missed you -
Thought of you, imagined what you were doing,
Prayed for you, prepared for you
As I made plans for your homecoming.

I missed you -
More so this year than those past.
Why? I'm not sure, but perhaps,
As time goes by at breathtaking speed,
I am forced to consider our human mortality.
Someday, I will miss you - or you will miss me -
As we reach beyond this world and gain eternity.
It doesn't matter who "goes first" as they say.
It matters what we do with our time together
Here and now.

Let us begin this New Year with fresh horizons in sight.
Let us explore together and find each other anew.
Let the quality of our lives be enriched
By the melding of our spirits.

Anticipation takes hold in my heart;
My mind can see you here with me again.
Welcome home, my love, welcome home, I'll say;
I missed you,
Oh how I missed you, my darling.

I'm Grateful

I'm grateful -
It's Sunday morning;
We've chosen this day as a day of rest.
A nice breakfast, discussion of current events,
Planning for the busy week ahead.
It seems we go, go, go and then,
As all things must,
We need to be still for a while.

It's raining, the sky is white -
Gray clouds moving, more rain in sight.
Could that be a hint of blue I see? No - I guess not.

The tick tock of the clock is mesmerizing.
The beat reminds me of a song:
Just A Closer Walk With Thee -
Grant it, Jesus, is my plea.
Daily walking close to Thee,
Let it be, dear Lord, let it be.
I sing while looking out the kitchen window.

On our 24th anniversary, just one month past,
We moved things around in the Great Room.
It has become the custom since our 20th year.
I like it. It gets better every year.

What gets better, you may ask,
The marriage or the Great Room?
Both, I answer. Not, of course, without turmoil.

Change is not easy for me, yet you seem to thrive on it.
Oh, well, that is changing too. We're learning -
Balance is the key.

For all the good things, Father, I'm thankful.
For health and strength, love, and family,
House and home. But, most of all,
For Hollis, my husband. Thank you.
I'm grateful.

You Touch Me

You touch me -
Deep in my soul you stir the yearnings of my womanhood.
Words cannot explain the hold you have
In the very core of my being;
Mere words cannot communicate.

You touch me -
Upheaval, consolation, your presence lifts me;
Lifts me higher than I ever dreamed possible.

You touch me -
When you risk showing the depth of your emotion;
Letting down the mask of so-called masculinity
And just being human.

You touch me -
When you write a love song,
Bring me a wild flower,

Or find just the right car for me.
You are my soulmate,
My husband,
My friend.
I am a better woman because -
You touch me.

You Still Touch Me

You still touch me -
After 25 years as husband and wife,
You still touch me -
Deep in the center of my being.

Simple things shared with you
Elevate them to a higher plane:
Coffee and a paper for two,
Singing a song in the car,
A bowl of your lentil soup,
The way of a man with a maid.

The house we live in has changed
And expanded over the years,
But the home we have created together
Remains a sure foundation - an anchor -
A safe haven.

When I look back and ponder where
We have been and how far we've come,

It is evident to me that our lives are
Part of a grand design.
I'm glad you chose me to be your wife,
Because, after 25 years,
You still touch me.

I Remember

I remember -
When you lovingly carried
One perfect tulip in your briefcase
From Oxford to London;
You surprised me, you did.

I remember -
When you stopped beside the road
To pick wild roses.

I remember -
The breathtakingly beautiful azalea
You placed on my windshield
So I would enjoy driving to work.

I remember -
How you took our first house
And transformed it from truly ugly into
The prettiest in the neighborhood.

I remember -

When we chose my first new car,
A 1976 gold Toyota Celica,
5 in the floor,
A sporty little car with class -
I felt special.
I remember -
When we drove that same car
On a whirlwind tour of the original 13 states
To celebrate the 200th year
Of our blessed country,
The United States of America.

I remember -
21 years later
When you presented me with
A green 1995 Dodge Neon Sport
With all the trimmings,
A little bit of heaven on wheels,
Complete with CD so I could hear Brian sing.

I remember -
Hearing the love in your voice
And seeing the passion in your face
As you talked about your sons,
Barton, the firstborn, and
Brian, the second gift;
Joy so deep it hurt.

I remember -
Arriving home to find you
Sitting at a beautiful piano,

A birthday gift that took me
Completely by surprise!

I remember -
Your longed-for dream
Of a house on Lone Mountain
Where you had so many memories
Of your Grandfather Green.
I pinch myself when I see
Evergreen Cottage a reality -
A respite from the world.
Thank you.

As in all relationships,
There are things I could remember -
But choose not to;
Things I could bring up that
Displeased me at the time.
But no, it's not worth it
To recall that you're not perfect.
My inner voice reminds me
Of my own faults; who am I
To bring up yours?

No, we've not always been
Happy with each other,
But we've been content -
O.K. most of the time, I concede.

As 27 years together draws near,
I sit here this night and -
I remember.

I Recall

It's been six years to the day,
I realized this a.m.
With paper and pen,
October 8, 2000, I remembered
The sweet things you did back when.
This day, October 8, 2006,
I recall how fast the journey has been.

October 1973, when first we met,
Your smile caught my eye;
Your sermons held my attention.
Humor and story you weaved with scripture:
Luke 10, The Good Samaritan,
How appropriate it is the one I remember.
Helping someone - oh, excuse me -
Assisting someone, you would prefer me to say.

You called and asked me out to lunch -
After that I had a hunch
Nothing would ever be the same.

As I sit at the table,
I can see you through the window
Sitting on the patio deck you recently built.
Searching for the tiny gold fish
You put in the little pond -
They are elusive - you are intent.
Watching them yesterday as they played and
Dined under the waterfall was fun.

The cool breeze of autumn was blowing,
Tinges of color peeking out.
It won't be long now, It won't be long -
The fireplace soon will be lit,
The trees will sing their song.

33 years now seem like the blink of an eye.
Slow down, Time, slow down, please.
Let us savor this phase of the journey;
Let us together make peace as friends.
How short, how short,
the journey has been!

Christmas 2007

Both your boys are here;
What a treat!
Christmas, twenty years past,
I recall, we planted a tree in Green Oaks Park -
It grows there still.

We may have a white Christmas,
some have said.
Wouldn't it be fun to whiz down the hill
On your blue sled?

You and I went shopping for gifts,
What fun!
You wanted to go to a particular place,
But, no, I wasn't sure.

Great gifts can be found there,
Said you, and so it was.
Quality, bargains, and so much more.

As I wrapped the gifts with tender care,
All spread out upon our bed,
Sweet thoughts were dancing in my head.
I placed them all around the tree you cut
And decorated with boughs of love.

Big sister, Betty,
A warm, soft, cloak, a beautiful red.
Baby sister, Sue,
A warm, soft, sleep outfit for her new bed.

Little Allister,
A kid's stool and your Sleepy Town Storybook,
nothing much.
Bart and Brian, you chose practical things -
Flashlights, tools, pillows, and such.

And, oh yes, I have a new CD player
Sitting next to my piano. Thanks, Babe,
So thoughtful and completely unexpected.

"Don't get me a gift", said you.
So, I figured out a way
To satisfy myself - and you.
I filled up your truck with gas - HA!
These days, quite a lot.
Wasn't I smart to think of that?

A warm fire, a warm hug, little fishes swimming ‘round;
Where on earth can better than this be found?

I love you, Hollis,
Merry Christmas ~

Gail

Appendix C

Notes

A Note on the Table

From Gail when she was going
Out of town to visit her Mother.

My Dearest Hollis,
Wind up the clock,
And pull out the stem.
The coffee is set for 7 AM.

Your clothes are prepared;
It's ready, set, go -
I love you a lot,
but that you already know.

A Note on the Mirror

From Hollis when he was going
Out of town on business.

UR loved,
Appreciated,
Liked,
Wanted,
And Admired.

Gail's Response To Hollis' Note

I found your note:
"U R loved,
Appreciated,
Liked,
Needed,
Wanted,
And Admired."

You covered all the bases.
A smile crossed my face;
The morning seemed brighter than before,
The duties of housework seemed lighter.
I looked forward to seeing you.

You also are loved, my dear;
Appreciated, my companion;
Liked, my friend;
Needed, my husband;

Wanted, my love;
And admired, my darling.

But there is another love
That transcends all of ours.
You are loved even more so by God,
Who dares to describe Himself
As your Heavenly Father.

As we celebrate 23 years as husband and wife,
and look back over the time,
I must say to you, no regrets.
I do not regret saying that one word
Which only you would understand.

It was a wise decision when I spoke that
Four letter word so full of promise,
Which inspired you to write a love song,
The first of many.

One little word -
I would say it again -

When.

Appendix D

PostScript

This is not the end....It is the beginning....
And I am going to enjoy every moment we share.

Why?

Because I love and "respect" you.
And that's for the record...

Hollis

Appendix E

Campus Crusade Recommended Reading List

LOC 2010925290

Downs, Tim and Downs, Joy (2003) Fight Fair: Winning at Conflict Without Losing at Love. Chicago: Moody Publishers.

Downs, Tim and Downs, Joy (2003) The Seven Conflicts: Resolving the Most Common Disagreements in Marriage. Chicago: Moody Press.

Eggerichs, Emerson (2004) Love and Respect. Nashville: Thomas Nelson, Inc.

Feldhahn, Shaunti and Feldhahn, Jeff (2006) For Men Only: A Straightforward Guide to the Inner Lives of Women. Atlanta: Veritas Enterprises, Inc.

Feldhahn, Shaunti (2004) For Women Only: What You Need to Know About the Inner Lives of Men. Atlanta: Veritas Enterprises, Inc.

Green, Hollis L. (2010), How To Build A Better Spouse Trap: How to choose a mate, learn from your mistakes, stay married, and teach others to break the cycle of dysfunctional relationships. Nashville: Global EdAdvancePRESS.

Harley, Willard F. (1986) His Needs, Her Needs: Building an Affair-Proof Marriage. Grand Rapids: Fleming H. Revell.

Lepine, Bob (1999) The Christian Husband. Ventura, CA: Regal Books.

Lewis, Robert and Hendricks, William (1991) Rocking the Roles. Colorado Springs: NavPress.

Rainey, Dennis (1989) Staying Close: Stopping the Natural Drift Toward Isolation in Marriage. Nashville: Thomas Nelson, Inc.

Rainey, Dennis and Rainey, Barbara (1995) Building Your Mate's Self-Esteem. Nashville: Thomas Nelson, Inc.

Rainey, Dennis and Rainey, Barbara (1995) Moments Together for Couples. Ventura, CA: Regal Books.

Rainey, Dennis and Rainey, Barbara (2000) Starting your Marriage Right: What you Need to Know and Do in the Early Years to Make it Last a Lifetime. Nashville: Thomas Nelson, Inc.

Sande, Kenneth (1991) The Peacemaker: A Biblical Guide to Resolving Personal Conflict. Grand Rapids: Baker Books.

Smalley, Gary T. (1979) For Better or Best. Grand Rapids: Zondervan.

Smalley, Gary T. (1979) If Only He Knew. Grand Rapids: Zondervan.

Walker, James (1989) Husbands Who Won't Lead and Wives Who Won't Follow: Help in Understanding your Mate, your Marriage, and your Expectations for Each Other. Minneapolis: Bethany House Publishers.

Wheat, Ed (1980) Love Life for Every Married Couple: How to Fall in Love, Stay in Love, Rekindle Your Love. Grand Rapids: Zondervan.

Wright, H. Norman (1960) *Communication: Key to your Marriage: A Practical Guide to a Creating a Happy, Fulfilling Relationship.* Ventura, CA: Regal Book

Appendix F

Bibliography and Selected Resources

Chapman, Gary, (1995) *The Five Love Languages: How to Express Heartfelt Commitment to Your Mate*. Chicago: Northfield Publishing.

Chapman, Audrey B. (2001) *Seven Attitude Adjustments for Finding a Loving Man*. New York: Pocket Books.

Coontz, Stephanie (2005). *Marriage, a History: From Obedience to Intimacy, or How Love Conquered Marriage*. Viking.

Cott, Nancy F. (2000). *Public Vows: A History of Marriage and the Nation*. Harvard University Press.

Dixon, Paricia and Osiris, Khalil (2002) *Talking and Listening with Care: A Communication Guide for Singles and Couples*.Dacatur, GA: Oji Publications.

Green, Hollis L. (2007) *Discipleship*. GlobalEdAdvancePress.

Green, Hollis L. (2008) *Fighting the Amalekites:* GlobalEdAdvancePress

Green, Hollis L. (2008) *Titanic Lessons:* GlobalEdAdvancePress

Green, Hollis L. (2009) *Remedial and Surrogate Parenting in the Custodial Arena:* GlobalEdAdvancePress.

Green, Hollis L. (2010) *The EVERGREEN Devotional New Testament:* PostGutenberg Books.

Gottman, John M. and Silver, Nan ,(1999) *The Seven Principles of Making Marriage Work* . New York: Three Rivers Press.

Howard J. Markman, Howard J., Stanley, Scott M. and Blumbert, Susan L. (2001) *Fighting for Your Marriage: Positive Steps for Preventing Divorce and Preserving a Lasting Love.* San Francisco: Jossey-Bass

July II, William (1998) *Brothers, Lust and Love: Thoughts on Manhood, Sex and Romance.* New York: Doubleday.

July II, William (1999) *Understanding the Tin Man: Why Do Many Men Avoid Intimacy.* New York: Double

Lewis, C. S., (1971). *The Four Loves*, New York: Harvest Books.

Whyte, M. K. (1990). *Dating, mating, and marriage.* Hawthorne, NY: Aldine de Gruyter.

Lucas, John (1998) *Conscious Marriage: From Chemistry to Communication* .Freedom, CA: The Crossing Press.

Norwood, Robin (1997) *Daily Meditations for Women Who Love Too Much.* New York: MJF Books.

Shumway, David R.(2003). *Modern Love, Romance, Intimacy, And the Marriage Crisis.* NY University Press.

Some, Sobonfu E. (1999) *Welcoming Sprit Home: Ancient African Teachings to Celebrate Children and Community.* .Novato, CA: New World Library.

Waite, Linda and Gallagher, Maggie, (2000) *The Case for Marriage: Why Married People are Happier, Healthier and Better Off Financially* .New York: Broadway Books.

Wile, D. B. (1993). *After the fight: A night in the life of a couple.* New York: Guilford Press.

Williams, R. (1989). *The trusting heart: Great news about Type A.* New York: Random House, Inc.

How To Build a Better Spouse Trap

ISBN 978-1-935434-45-0

Hollis L. Green, ThD, PhD

a division of
GlobalEdAdvancePress

www.ingramcontent.com/pod-product-compliance
Lightning Source LLC
LaVergne TN
LVHW010059110826
845155LV00028B/413

* 9 7 8 1 9 3 5 4 3 4 4 5 0 *